By this time, Gillian was so lost in her memories, she barely noticed him. "I always liked the Perseids the best," she said. "And not just because it's the biggest one. Dad told me it was named after Perseus because all the meteors in that shower appear to come from that constellation. I always liked Perseus," she said. "'The Hero.' I liked the legend."

Max's eyes twinkled as he watched her face light up. "You really are a romantic at heart, aren't you?" His voice was soft and low.

Palisades.
Pure Romance.

FICTION THAT FEATURES CREDIBLE CHARACTERS AND

ENTERTAINING PLOT LINES, WHILE CONTINUING TO UPHOLD

STRONG CHRISTIAN VALUES. FROM HIGH ADVENTURE

TO TENDER STORIES OF THE HEART, EACH PALISADES

ROMANCE IS AN UNDILUTED STORY OF LOVE,

FROM BEGINNING TO END!

A PALISADES CONTEMPORY
ROMANCE

Stardust

SHARI MACDONALD

PALISADES

This is a work of fiction. The characters, incidents, and dialogues are products of the author's imagination and are not to be construed as real. Any resemblance to actual events or persons, living or dead, is entirely coincidental.

STARDUST
published by Palisades
a part of the Questar publishing family

© 1997 by Shari MacDonald
International Standard Book Number: 1-57673-109-X

Cover illustration by Chris Hopkins
Cover designed by Brenda McGee
Edited by Traci DePree

Most scripture quotations are from:
The Holy Bible, New International Version (NIV) © 1973, 1984 by
International Bible Society, used by permission of Zondervan Publishing House.

Printed in the United States of America

For information:
QUESTAR PUBLISHERS, INC.
POST OFFICE BOX 1720
SISTERS, OREGON 97759

LIBRARY OF CONGRESS CATALOGING-IN-PUBLICATION DATA
MacDonald, Shari.
    Stardust / by Shari MacDonald.
        p. cm.
    ISBN 1-57673-109-X (alk. paper)
    I. Title.
PS3563.A2887S7   1997   97-6687
813'.54--dc21   CIP

97 98 99 00 01 02 03 04 — 10 9 8 7 6 5 4 3 2 1

To my brother, Daniel Patrick MacDonald.
For loving the stars and the heavens and
the One who made them...
and for loving me.

Thanks for the great memories of stargazing together
when we were kids, and
for having the patience to let your little sister use
your telescope (sometimes).
Only for you would I have braved the flying bats.

Special thanks

To Michael Bakich, Ph.D., for setting me straight on all the things I thought I knew about astronomy, and for helping me out with the countless things I didn't. E-mails even during Christmas vacation? Like God's, your mercies are never ceasing.

To Claire Widmark, for moving to New Jersey and opening my eyes to how beautiful it is, though it doesn't make up for missing you.

To Allen Jones and Beth Reilley for making sure *my* New Jersey sounds like the *real* New Jersey.

To my editor, Traci DePree, for your tremendous help and support.

And to my previous editors, Judith Markham and Gloria Chisholm, because I unbelievably forgot to give public thanks for your wonderful work on my first three books.

*The heavens tell of the glory of God and
the firmament tells the work of his hands.*

PSALM 19:1

Prologue

May 4, 1975

"Look, Mama!" Wide hazel eyes shone bright with hope as the child tipped back her curly, golden head and peered up at the vast New Jersey sky. "It's the first star!" the girl whispered in awe and reached out one red-mittened paw to tug at her mother's sleeve.

Lovingly, Emma wrapped one hand around her daughter's fingers. "I see it, Gilly!" she murmured, throwing a halfhearted glance heavenward but continuing to walk wearily toward the house.

Normally, she might stop for a moment to enjoy the sights, smells, and sounds that were so much a part of the Central New Jersey country experience. But not tonight. It had been a long evening of "networking" with her husband's associates at the university. Joseph had promised they would be home by eight; they hadn't even pulled into the driveway until nine-thirty. If she'd suspected it was going to be more than a simple dinner, and an evening-long affair at that, she would have tried to get a baby-sitter. Amazingly, Gilly had weathered the evening well. Better, in fact, than Emma had. Nevertheless, it was time to get this little girl—and this woman—to bed.

The gloved hand slipped from her grasp as Gillian resolutely planted her feet against the pavement and declared, "I gotta make a wish!" Patiently, Emma Spencer waited as her only child screwed her face up tight and began to whisper in a singsong voice, "Star light, star bright, first start I see tonight, I wish I may, I wish I might, have this wish I wish tonight. I wish…" She fell silent then, but her lips continued to move soundlessly.

"Gillian, hurry up," Joseph called out crossly from several feet ahead. He gave his wife a look of disapproval. "You know, you really shouldn't encourage her in these things. She's just going to get her hopes up, thinking her wishes will come true." Without waiting for an answer, he turned and stepped up to the wraparound porch with keys in hand, while Emma stopped and waited for Gilly to finish.

When she opened her eyes again, the little girl's face was shining.

Emma leaned down, with her face close to Gillian's. "What did you wish for, sweetheart?" she asked with a smile and smoothed the fabric of her child's bright red coat.

"Oh no, Mama." Gilly shook her head fiercely. "I can't tell you. Then it won't come true."

The woman's lips twitched in amusement. "Are you sure, honey? I thought that rule was just for blowing out birthday candles."

"We-ell…" Gillian eyed her uncertainly. Then, her desire to share the secret overcoming her resolve, she made a decision. "Okay!" she beamed. "I wished for a husban' who will love me," she said confidently. "Like Raggedy Anne has Raggedy Andy, Barbie has Ken…and you have Daddy!"

Emma gave her a halfhearted smile. "Well! I'm honored to be in such illustrious company," she said weakly.

Gilly scowled, as if disapproving her mother's choice of big words, but allowed herself to be swept up in a warm, motherly hug.

"That should be an easy wish to make come true," Emma said, holding her tightly. "You're pretty lovable, you know."

"Do you think the stars can hear me when I wish?" Gilly asked, wriggling within her mother's arms.

"I don't know," Emma replied thoughtfully, letting her own gaze drift to the sky overhead. "But my mother—your grandma—always told me that God can."

Gilly searched her mother's face. "Does that mean my wish will come true?" she asked after a moment of careful consideration.

"I don't know," Emma repeated, but her eyes seemed hopeful, too. "I guess we'll just have to wait and see, honey," she said, pressing her lips against her child's soft, fragrant golden hair. "We'll just have to wait and see."

One

To Noon he fell, from Noon to dewy Eve,
A Summer's day; and with the setting Sun
Dropt from the Zenith like a falling Star.
JOHN MILTON, PARADISE LOST

June 19, 1987

From my window I can see him, just sitting there, drinking from a big ol' tumbler of Mom's horrible sun tea. He's at the patio table she bought last summer, the one with the ocean-colored beach umbrella sticking out of the Plexiglass top. Painted butterflies flap across the material, which drapes over his head like a tacky plastic sky. I'd have thought Dad wouldn't be caught dead under anything so froufrou, but I learned a long time ago that he doesn't notice anything he doesn't want to. Not even me.

Yesterday he missed my birthday...again. Something about a black hole lecture this time. Isn't that perfect? What I want to know is, what kind of pathetic nerd goes to an astrophysics seminar on June 18, anyway? It's summer vacation, for crying out loud. You'd think these guys would take a break sometimes, but they never do.

Take right now, for instance. He could be off playing golf, like Jenny's father, or setting up a barbecue, if we had one. But what's my dad doing? Waiting around for one of his eager-beaver students from the university. He takes one under his wing every year, and this time he's picked some hot-shot grad student, a math whiz from Idaho. Guys like that are always trying to buddy-up to him. Mom calls it

15

"mentoring." I call it "sucking up." Dad's students know he's friends with important scientists all over the world. They want to milk it for all it's worth. And Dad, he doesn't even see or care that he's being used.

My theory is, he just likes having all these guys around, acting like they worship him. It makes him feel important, though you'd think he would feel important enough already. I don't worship Dad anymore, and he knows it. Not that it mattered when I did. Sometimes I think things would have been different if I'd been a boy, although I'm not sure why. All I know is, Dad somehow makes time for these twerpy little geeks, but he's never, ever had time for me. Not since I was little, anyway. I'm glad I don't worship him. I'd be crazy if I did.

Mom says Dad really loves me, he's just obsessed with his own little science world, and it's hard for him to see how the things he does affect those of us living in reality. Single-minded, she calls it. Mom's got words for everything. So do I, but I'm not allowed to use them. Mom's very devout. She became a Christian last year, so she's got a lot of rules now about how I'm supposed to behave. I believe in God, too. Sort of. I'm just not all gung ho about it, like Mom is. Most of her rules are okay, though. I mean, I'd never say this to her, but at least she's paying attention to how I live my life, which is a lot more than I can say about Dad.

This year's birthday was better than last year's, though, I have to admit. Dad promised to come to my party, then didn't even show. No Dad, no present. Nada. This year, at least there were a bunch of packages from him. "To Gilly," they said, in Mom's loopy handwriting. "Love, Dad." I'm not dumb—I know Mom bought them. She didn't even try to hide it. But at least she made the effort, so we could all pretend he wanted to be there. That was a relief.

One of the presents, it turned out, was this diary. I think Mom misses being young. Lately, she's been telling me that I'm in the prime of my life. That's why she got me this book, I guess. So I can write down all the prime stuff that happens to me. Puhlleeeeeze. Who does she think she's kidding? I can't think of even one thing that's ever happened to me that's so exciting I'd want to remember it forever. Except maybe that time in third grade when Jamie Kubitz bit my arm, and I turned around and bit him right back. You could see teeth marks on his knuckles for almost a week. That was pretty cool. I think I'd like to remember that forever. I bet you Jamie would rather forget.

Mom says I should write about me, who I am, what I think. That seems kinda dumb. I'm writing this for me, aren't I? Don't I know who I am? But maybe I'll die, like Anne Frank. Then I guess I might become famous, as long as people know who I am and why they should care about me. So, here goes.

I'm Gillian Spencer, fifteen—oops, no, now I'm sixteen years old. My dad is the very famous Dr. Joseph Spencer, professor of astrophysics at Princeton University. Mother is Emma Masterson-Spencer, political speech writer. If it sounds like it would be cool to have two famous parents…well, it's not. Dad says that lots of kids would appreciate having distinguished parents. I say, goody for them. The only advantage I can see is that Mom and Dad can afford to buy me rad clothes and stuff, which isn't such an advantage at my school anyway. Everyone at Chatsworth has rich parents and expensive clothes. So, really, the only effect my parents' jobs have on me is that they take Mom and Dad away for a few days every month. At least I have our housekeeper, Norrie. I can always count on her to be here. Last summer, one of my aunts was visiting and she called Norrie my nanny. Anyone with any sense knows that a fifteen-year-old doesn't need a baby-sitter! Norrie, at least, understood. "Oh no," she shook her gray head and looked at me seriously. "That girl doesn't need a nanny, she needs a friend." Amen to that, sister.

Not that I don't have friends, mind you. I may not be the most popular girl at Chatsworth, but I have a pretty tight circle of girls I hang with. Some of the teachers think I don't try very hard at my studies, and I guess that's true. Everyone at Chat is just so competitive. I hate it. All the kids have rich, smart parents. Dad says I'll have to try harder if I want to get into a good college. Maybe I'd care about that more if I knew what I wanted to do. Dad's pushing me toward astronomy. Big surprise. It's true, I really liked watching the stars with him when I was a kid, but that was a long time ago. Sometimes I still go out and look at the sky, but if Dad sees me, I stop and pretend I'm out picking up my bike or something. I don't want him to feel too smug. He hasn't got my loyalty. He hasn't earned it.

Speaking of Dad, he's still out there, by the way, and looking pretty ticked. I guess the kid is late. That's something, anyhow. It's good for my father, I think, to have things not go the way he plans every once in a while. That way he knows what it's like. Like this one time—

Oh, wait. Here comes the geek. This should be good. Okay...he just poked his bushy brown head in the side gate, and now Dad's waving him in. But...you know, the funny thing is, this one doesn't really look like a geek. In fact, he's dressed pretty cool. No dopey little white button-up shirt or polyester pants. Just a navy sweatshirt and jeans. His hair is awfully thick, but it's actually kind of cute. This has gotta be a mistake. He can't be one of Dad's weirdo students. Wait...he's starting to turn around now, and...oh, my gosh, this one is a babe! And now he's shaking my dad's hand like he knows him, and Dad is smiling and pointing toward the house, and the guy just looked up, and I think he saw me before I could duck, 'cause he smiled real big, right at my window!

Okay, that's it. I've got to go call Jenny! More later...Finally, I've got something to write about! Maybe this is going to be a cool summer after all.

June 14, 1997

"Hey, Bridget! Look at me! I'm Julia Child!" Gleefully, twenty-six-year-old Gillian Spencer raised two eggs high over the kitchen stove—holding one in each hand—and eyed her cast-iron pan, which was already sizzling invitingly. Her hazel eyes danced as she considered the feat she was about to attempt.

"Uhnh," her roommate mumbled noncommittally, keeping her brown eyes trained on the newspaper in front of her. "Just make sure you don't drop the eggs on the burner again, please."

Gillian scowled in disappointment but dutifully lowered her arms. "You didn't even bother to look up," she grumbled, throwing a disparaging look at Bridget. "I was going to crack 'em with both hands at once." She narrowed her eyes at a dark spot on one egg shell, shrugged, and dismissed it, having decided it was simply a bit of dried goo that had gotten stuck while in the carton.

From the breakfast nook, tucked into the west corner of the old farmhouse kitchen, Bridget read the paper while nursing a lukewarm cup of coffee. "Yeah, well, I don't stop at the scene of accidents, either." A tiny smile played at the corner of her lips. "There are some things I'd just rather not witness. Like you cooking."

She looked up at Gillian, but Gillian was ignoring her. Having taken Bridget's chastisement to heart, she let her eyes flicker across the sunlit room, looking for a surface other than the pan upon which to crack her eggs. At last her gaze settled back on the edge of the stove. "Ah-ha!" she cried triumphantly.

"Good grief," Bridget said. "What are you doing now?" Then, as realization dawned on her, "Oh no. Gil, wait. Now, don't do that, you'll—!"

"Whoops!" Gilly froze, her hands poised in midair, as two yellow yolks and a clear, gooey mass dribbled down the crack between the battered white stove and the old Amana refrigerator. She chuckled despite herself. Bridget laid the paper down and began to giggle uncontrollably.

"What's going on?" The soft voice of their third roommate, Pam Holzman, could barely be heard over the din of their laughter. Pam padded into the room, wearing her gray cotton pj's and thick, oversized wool socks. "Oh," she said, her bright blue eyes inspecting the mess. "I see Gillian has been cooking again. I thought we made a rule against that." She tucked a strand of her long, black hair behind one ear and began digging in the painted white cupboard for a box of her favorite sugar-coated cereal.

"Well, excuse me for trying to eat something healthy." Gillian sniffed self-righteously, trying to divert the attention from her own faux pas. "At least I'm not scarfing down Sugar-O's, or whatever you call that junk you eat." She wiped egg from her hands with a terry cloth dish towel. Thankfully, she had managed not to spill any on her shirt of lilac-colored linen or on her trim white cotton pants.

Pam yawned and continued her search, undeterred by Gillian's criticism. "Healthy? I don't think so. A little sugar isn't going to clog my arteries," she patiently explained. "Unlike *your* breakfast. I'm surprised at you. You should know better. You're supposed to be a scientist, you know. Doesn't that mean anything nowadays?"

Gillian sighed. "An egg every now and then isn't going to hurt me, and the protein's good for me. Anyway, I *like* real food. I'd never survive on that stuff you eat—which, by the way, isn't as harmless as you think—or on nothing but coffee, like Bridget."

At the sound of her name, Bridget threw her arms up in the air. "I am *not* going to have this conversation." She shook her head of short chestnut curls. "When we moved in together, we agreed not to mother each other. Remember?" Despite her breakfasts of coffee, Bridget still looked healthy and well-fed but by no means overweight. Actually, she was quite attractive. And even though she hadn't yet met the man of her dreams—though not for lack of trying—her looks had brought her more than a few dates over the years. This morning, Gillian noticed, Bridget looked especially nice, with her cocoa-colored cotton pants and matching short-sleeved cable cardigan bringing out the rich color in her deep, brown eyes.

"Yeah, Gillian. Which means, I'm not going to clean up your mess." Pam stared at the dripping egg goo, which was already beginning to mold itself to the black and white vinyl floor tiles.

"Okay, okay. I get the picture." Gillian rested her hands on her slim hips and regarded the situation with a problem-solver's eye. Then, choosing a plan of action, she leaned forward over the counter, secured the fingers of both hands behind the back corner of the fridge, and began to carefully jog the appliance forward.

"Oh, Gil. You're never going to get it out that way!" Bridget abandoned her newspaper and moved to help her. Within minutes, the two women had pulled it from its corner. As she reclaimed her spot at the breakfast nook, Bridget wiped away a bit of dust that clung to her sleeve.

"Thanks." Gillian went to the sink, retrieved a damp sponge, and set to work. Before long, the spill was gone, the refrigerator back in position, and the egg fiasco nothing more than a memory. "There!" she said, with a little sigh of satisfaction. "Now, let's see...let me try this again." But by this time the frying pan was a blackened mess, having burned up the oil coating she had sprayed inside it. "Ugh." She turned off the stove in disgust, grabbed a bowl and spoon, and seated herself at the table next to Pam. "May I?" she said, nodding at the box of frosted oat cereal.

"Hmm." Pam pretended to consider her request. "Are you sure you can *survive* on this stuff?"

"I'm sure," Gillian told her seriously, refusing to rise to the bait.

"No more mocking my breakfast?" her roommate pressed.

Gillian sighed again. "Oh, all right. If you insist. No more mocking."

"Okay," Pam said cheerfully, pushing the box toward her. "Help yourself."

Gillian grabbed the box, drawing her eyebrows together in consternation as she poured. "Seriously, though, you guys...do you really think I'm such a bad cook?"

"What do you mean?" Bridget glanced up from her paper. "Why does it matter what *we* think? The question is, do *you* think you're a bad cook?"

"No-oo," Gillian said uncertainly. "I know I'm kind of disorganized—"

"You mean you cook like the Absentminded Professor," Pam said helpfully.

"—and I have a tendency toward minor accidents," Gillian continued, ignoring her. "But I think the food winds up tasting okay."

"Well, then. What's the problem?"

"We-ell..."

Bridget waved her coffee spoon in the air, and with the expression of a psychiatrist on the verge of a clinical breakthrough said, "Keith hates your cooking. That's it, isn't it?"

Gillian smiled at the reference to her boyfriend. Blond, brilliant, full of smiles...No, Keith wasn't her problem. The two of them never fought. Theirs was an easy partnership, one that centered around social functions and mutual cheerleading. He supported her one-hundred percent in her career goals and ambitions, and she supported him. It never occurred to her to criticize him or to challenge him—they didn't have that kind of relationship. Gillian was sure Keith felt the same way.

She shook her head. "Huh-unh. He likes my cooking just fine."

"Well, then...?"

"Oh, it's nothing." Gillian dragged her spoon through her bowl, playing with the floating O's. "Forget it."

"Speaking of Keith, doesn't he come home sometime this week? Aren't you excited about seeing him?" Bridget smiled knowingly, the previous subject already forgotten, and Gillian grinned in return.

Leave it to Bridget to bring the conversation back to romance. Like Gillian, she was a graduate student at Princeton. But unlike Gil, who studied astrophysics, Bridget pursued not science, but Romance Literature. Gillian theorized that at some point, Bridget's studies had seeped into some deeper part of her psyche—there was nothing more interesting to the woman than romance, and nothing she desired more for her own life than love. In some individuals, this characteristic would seem irritating, even pathetic. In Bridget, it was somehow endearing.

"Yes, I'm excited. Of course I am," Gillian told Bridget logically. "He's been away at this legal conference for over a week. I've missed him a lot." She felt a tiny twinge of guilt at the sound of her words. Was that last part a white lie? The truth of the matter was, she had almost been *relieved* to have a week to herself. That didn't mean anything significant, though, she was sure. Lots of couples—*happy* couples—needed to take time for themselves as individuals. Enjoying their time apart didn't mean a thing. She *did* miss Keith…sort of. It was always nice to have him around. It was just…just that she had been so busy lately. She wasn't quite ready to give up her freedom yet. She'd gotten more done during his absence than she normally did in a month. But, she reminded herself, work wasn't everything.

She had broken up, for one reason or another, with countless men since she had been at Princeton. One guy talked too much, another talked too little…. It seemed there was always something that eventually got under her skin and caused her to break up. At this rate, she'd be alone forever. Gillian was determined to hang in there this time.

She would feel more excited, she was sure, once she saw Keith at the airport. He was the nicest guy she had ever dated. She wasn't going to mess this one up, just because there weren't incredible sparks. Sometimes love just wasn't the walk in the park folks expected. Gillian had felt sparks once before, back when she was barely more than a kid, and the feeling hadn't been returned. There wasn't anything very romantic about *that*.

"He's such a *cutie*, Gil. How can you stand it?" Bridget said plaintively, her thoughts clearly still on Keith. "Why can't I ever meet—oh!" She sat up straight. "I almost forgot! Speaking of *cuties*, who's that gorgeous new guy in your department?"

"What new guy?" Gillian lowered her eyes and dug into her bowl of now-soggy oat bits. She knew exactly who Bridget was talking about. How could she *not*? She'd been avoiding him all week.

"Tasty little morsels, aren't they?" Pam couldn't help but tease. Gillian grimaced but didn't feel much like mocking anymore.

"You know," Bridget said impatiently, ignoring their sparring. "The *new* one. The one without a wedding ring. I saw him yesterday when I dropped off your gym bag. You were at lunch, and I saw him talking with your nerdy boss."

"You mean Ed Cheatham?"

"That's the one. Ed was saying something about finding this guy an office to work in."

Gillian stuck another spoonful of cereal into her mouth and chewed, seizing upon the extra moment to collect her thoughts. *So, Bridget's seen him. I wonder what he looks like now?* After ten years, she was more than a little curious. Not curious enough, though, to stick around the main office where he might run across her. She felt silly avoiding the man. But she'd spent years getting over the crush she'd had on Max Bishop, and she wasn't exactly looking forward to having those old memories come up again. She certainly didn't want *anyone* to know about how pitifully infatuated—and rejected—she had been.

"I have no idea who he is, Bridget," she fibbed.

"Well, do you think you could find out?"

Gillian stared at her. "Why? Are you interested or something?"

"Um, I don't know," her friend backpedaled a bit, her face flushing pink with embarrassment. "I mean, he's cute and everything, but I don't really know hi—"

"Oh, give it up, Bridget. It's too late to play coy now," Pam informed her. "It's *obvious* you like the guy."

"That's not necessarily true." Bridget tried to sound disinterested. "I don't know anything about him. Besides, maybe Gillian's holding out on me. Maybe she knows all about him and is just keeping him for herself."

"Oh, right! That's me. A guy in every port!" Gillian protested, pasting a smile on her face. "No thanks. I've got my hands full already with Keith. You can have the new guy, if you want. I'll see what I can find out about him." Suddenly, Gillie felt sick. She peered into the blue bowl in front of her. *The milk must be bad. I'd better remember to check the date....*

"Thanks, Gil!" Bridget sat back and smiled in relief. "Hey, do you want to forget your gym bag again?" she tried hopefully. "I can bring it by one more time."

"Hmm. Very subtle. I'm sure no one would notice." Gillian said in a weak attempt to tease her. "I think I've got a better idea, though. How about this? You come down and meet me for lunch. I'll arrange to be running late so you can hang around for a few minutes. That way you can meet the guy." She sat back in her chair, her queasiness fading to smugness. *That's it,* she told herself. *Set Max up with Bridget!* It was perfect. After a move like that, no one—not even Gillian, herself—could doubt that she was over him.

"Thanks, Gil. You're the best!" Bridget swallowed the dregs of her cold coffee, made a face, and cleared her things from the table. "Oh, my gosh, look at the time. You want to carpool? I have to go in early today."

"Nah, thanks." Gillian shook her head. "I have no idea how late I'll have to stay tonight. I'll just see you this afternoon."

"Okay."

As the two prepared to head off to the university, Pam grabbed the paper and pawed through the pages, as part of her daily search through the want ads.

"Got any interviews today?" Gillian asked.

"Nope. Still figuring out what I want to do next," Pam said, referring to her recent graduation from Princeton's MBA program.

"Ugh." Bridget eyed Pam with disgust. "I can't *believe* you get to stay home all day."

"Sorry, sweetie!" Pam batted her eyelashes, looking not the least bit apologetic. "I have a feeling you've got a more exciting day ahead, though."

"That's right, Bridget," Gillian agreed, wondering what the day might hold. "You met a cute guy. Who knows? This might turn out to be an interesting summer, after all."

Two

This is the very ecstasy of love.
SHAKESPEARE, *AS YOU LIKE IT* (III, II)

June 25, 1987

I've been spying on this guy for almost a week now. He seemed so great at first, I was sure that there had to be some mistake. So I watched him reeeaaallly carefully. Any minute, I figured, his geek tendencies would begin to show. I looked for pocket protectors, but he carries his pens around in his notebook, just like the rest of us. I checked out the hem of his pants, but they weren't high-waters. He doesn't wear polyester, either. And on his feet he wears regular old athletic shoes, like a normal guy. Is he for real? How'd he end up in one of my dad's classes?

He's come to see my father three times now. During the school year, Dad's grad students don't show their faces so much around the house. But during the summer, Dad likes to make them come here. It's a power thing, I guess. I still don't get to see this one a lot, though. He usually goes straight to Dad's study. If I wasn't watching for him, I'd miss him altogether.

One day I actually gathered up the nerve to ask Dad about him. It was totally underhanded, the way I did it. Quite a work of art, though Mom would never approve. Dad was in his office on Tuesday morning, working on some papers, when I knocked on the door.

27

I leaned on the doorjamb, all casual-like. "Um…some guy called for you this morning, but I forgot to write down the message," I told him. "Sorry."

Dad didn't even look up. "Well, who was it?" he asked.

"I—I don't remember."

"Did you recognize the voice? Was it one of the professors at the university?"

"Nooooo," I said slowly, pretending like I was trying to remember. "He sounded younger than that. Coulda been one of your students. I'm pretty sure I'd recognize the name if I heard it again." Then I set my final trap: "Could be that new guy you're tutoring."

Dad didn't answer at first, and for a sickening moment, I was afraid he wasn't going to. Then finally he lifted his head. "What's that?" he asked. "Tutoring? Do you mean Max Bishop?"

I chewed on my thumbnail and played dumb. "I dunno. That doesn't really sound familiar. Are you the advisor for more than one student right now?"

"No, just Max."

"The one who's been coming here to the house?" I must have sounded a little too interested because Dad gave me a funny look right then.

"Yes. Max is the young man who has been coming here. Are you saying that he called?"

"Uh…no. I'm sure that wasn't it. Must have been some other guy. I guess he'll call back if it's important. See ya." Then I got out of there as fast as I could.

What's going on with me? I mean, I've noticed guys in my class before. And even though I've never known one I liked that much, I've always kinda enjoyed the idea. But…I've never felt anything like this before. No wonder people say that love makes you sick. I'm getting queasy just thinking about it.

Max Bishop…Max Bishop…Max Bishop. I like writing the name. I like watching him even better. I've figured out that I have a pretty good line of vision from my bedroom window. Dad's office has a door at the side of the house, and to get to it you have to walk through the backyard. I always liked this before, because if I knew the geeks were coming, it made it easier to avoid them. Now that there aren't any geeks, it's a pain. See, if Max had to come to the front door of the house, I could answer it and see him up close. The way it is now, though, at least I get a good look at him when he comes into the yard.

I'm not sure what it is about him that makes him so...watchable. Maybe it's the way he moves: all smooth and confident, but full of tension and energy at the same time—like a tiger prowling the desert, looking for his next meal, even though he's not quite ready to eat it. It's not that Max looks uptight. He seems relaxed...sort of. His arms swing easily from his shoulders, and he's got a confident, athletic walk that's nothing like the puny little steps my dad's students usually take. But there's a fire in his eyes. I can see it from all the way up here.

One day, my dad was walking Max out to the gate after their session, and they were arguing about something. I remember, I looked down and Max's eyes were just snapping! I've never been able to quite tell what color they are, but at that moment they were bright and black, like the shells of two beetles. His voice was raised in excitement, and he waved his arms like crazy. I wished right then that I had paid more attention when Dad talked at the dinner table about his work. I wanted to know what made this guy feel so passionate. What made him tick. Dad, too. Suddenly, it seemed really important to understand.

That was a couple of days ago. But then this morning, it happened....I finally got to talk to Max face-to-face!

He had been in his session with Dad for about a half hour, with another half hour to go. Mom had just called me downstairs to help her peel carrots for dinner. It's Norrie's day off, and Mom hates getting stuck in the kitchen all by herself. So I was down there, peeling and pouting because I wasn't going to get to see Max leave, when Mom realized she didn't have enough potatoes. So I volunteered to run to the store. I figured I was going to miss Max anyway. There wasn't any point in sticking around here.

Mom gave me some money, and I went out to get my bike. All I can say is, thank goodness I got a new one last year. (I'm old enough to get my driver's license now, but Dad hasn't given me permission to drive yet. I think he likes having me stay dependent upon him and Mom. Don't even get me started on that whole issue....) The ugly, babyish, hot pink bike, with its basket and tassels and banana seat, was tucked safely in the back of the garage. I had just climbed on my fire-red ten-speed and turned it toward the road when I heard someone come up behind me and say, "Hey, nice bike."

I looked up, and it was Max! What was he doing out here? I didn't know what to say. How would a girl his age answer a comment like that? I opened my mouth to say something flirty, like, "Thanks. Nice eyes." They were, too. Really intense, this great dark blue. But instead it came out: "Ummmm…thanks, I got it for my birthday." Oh no, I thought. Now he's going to ask me how old I am. And, of course, he did.

"Seventeen," I lied, then immediately felt guilty. Mom hates it when I stretch the truth. It seemed like an even bigger sin to be lying to him.

"Really?" he said. "You're not Gillian then? Dr. Spencer said he had a daughter who just turned sixteen." Max had me there. He could have been really mean about it, but I'm sure he didn't embarrass me on purpose. At first, I thought he really believed I was someone else. But then I saw the twinkle in his eye, and I realized he knew the truth. He was just making me come clean.

"Oh. Uh, no. That's me. Sorry. I thought you were asking how old I was…uh, inside. You know, in my heart. If you want actual calendar years, I'm sixteen." I tried to make a joke of it, but I thought I might choke on my words. The guy caught me lying. I was sure he would give me a look of total disgust. But instead, he actually laughed. I guess he appreciated my talent for making up creative excuses. If only he knew how much practice I've had, maybe it wouldn't have seemed so cute.

"No kidding?" he said. "Hunh. Well, in my heart I think I'm sixteen." That's when I began to melt. "It's a great age. You wear it well," he said. I wasn't sure what he meant by that, but I hoped it was some kind of compliment.

For a moment, neither one of us said anything. Then I couldn't stand it anymore. I had to say something. "What are you doing out here?" I blurted out. Immediately, I wanted to kick myself. I talked like a kid. It sounded like I didn't even want him around. What was wrong with me?

"Your dad got an important call, so I took off early," Max told me. I thought I must look like I was about to fall over, but he didn't even notice that my mind was swirling. "Maybe we'll make up the time next week." He grinned at me. "So, I guess I'll see you?" And then he turned around and walked away, right down the street.

And...I know it sounds dopey, but I swear, he took my heart with him. Just like those romance books say. He really did.

June 14, 1997

"No, no, nooooooooo!" Gillian cried in anguish. "Don't crash, you beast!" she begged the computer, but her words were futile. After an instant-long power surge that sent lines zigzagging across her screen, it was clear that the figures she'd been analyzing for over an hour were gone.

Exhaling slowly, she pulled her long, honey-colored hair back into a makeshift knot and secured it with two pencils. *I should have known better. I should have saved my document.* The thought hadn't even occurred to her, she'd been so engrossed in her work. Most of the computers in the physics department were set up with surge protectors to guard against any power shifts. Unfortunately, her temporary workstation in the break room lacked such a luxury.

Gillian sighed. Sometimes being a grad student was a real pain—she managed to get all the grunt work. For the last couple of weeks, she'd been stuck in the department's only unoccupied space, sorting through stacks of documents that needed analysis. No other office had been available. At least the assignment kept her out of the main office during the week of Max's arrival. But that was the *only* good thing about it. She had been hoping for months that Ed would assign her to some interesting project. All she'd done over the past year was a little bit of number crunching, a lot of paper pushing, and a truckload of filing. Though there weren't any classes this summer, she was to continue working in the department until the fall semester began.

Gillian stared at the empty screen. "Well, that's one hour out of my life I'll never see again." She grumbled and looked at her watch. "Uh-oh. Almost lunch time." She wasn't looking forward to this one bit. At some point, though, she was going to have to face Max. Besides, Bridget was meeting her at one o'clock, and so far Gillian hadn't accomplished any part of her mission. When she had arrived that morning, the "new guy" and Ed had been nowhere to be seen. She'd just have to hope, for Bridget's sake, that at least one of them was back by now.

Thankfully, when she returned to the main office, Ed's inbox was empty—a sure sign that he had recently collected his ever-growing stack of messages. This suspicion was confirmed when she found him in his office, wearing his customary button-up dress shirt, gray slacks, and running shoes. She blinked and tried to ignore the obvious fashion "don't."

"Morning, Gillian." Ed's greeting was polite enough, but he didn't bother to take his feet down from their place of rest on his metal desk. Gillian didn't mind. Ed was a brilliant physicist, even if he lacked the most basic of social skills. She had long ago ceased to take his slights personally. He was rude to every one of the grad students. If it sometimes seemed like he was particularly indifferent to her, she knew this was simply because her eagerness to get rolling on a meaty project could be irritating to even the most gracious of souls.

"Hey, Ed." Gillian glanced at the only other chair in the room—a hard, vinyl-and-metal affair, piled high with textbooks. She didn't feel comfortable moving the stack, and Ed didn't offer, so she remained standing.

"How are those calculations coming?" Ed looked up at her and chewed on the metal end of his pencil. The eraser was already gone. Gillian couldn't help wondering if he had accidentally swallowed it.

She hesitated before answering. "Oh, not so bad, I guess, overall. I'm running behind this morning, though," she finally told him. "The computer crashed for a second, and I lost an hour's worth of work." There, she'd said it. She watched him for a reaction, but, surprisingly, Ed didn't seem as concerned about it as she'd feared.

"Oh, well. You can make it up later," he said easily. "I've got something else I want you to do this afternoon, anyway."

"You do?" Gillian shifted her feet uncomfortably and tried to keep the sound of dread from her voice. What was it this time? Purging the department's files from the 1950s? Inputting a notebook full of someone else's calculations? If *she* was getting the assignment, it couldn't be good. Ed hadn't given her a prime project *yet*.

"That's right." Ed stared at her expectantly, as if waiting for her to sit down and hear the details. Gillian glanced once more at the chair across from him but remained standing. Ed hadn't ever gone out of his way to make things easy for her. She wasn't going to act like an overeager schoolgirl. Manner-impaired or not, if he wanted her to sit down, he could very well make room for her. Finally, his eyes followed hers, and with a look of exasperation, he stood and removed the offending books. "Thanks." Gillian seized the unspoken invitation and took a seat.

"I'm sure you've heard," Ed went on as he settled back into his own chair, "that we have a new research astronomer on board, starting this week." Gillian purposely kept her expression blank. "He's a specialist in quantum cosmology. Now, I know that's your area of interest."

Gillian nodded. It was. Ever since she was a child, she had been intrigued by the night sky—the stars, the planets...the asteroids, meteors, and comets. In recent years, her thoughts had turned increasingly to where it had all come from. After centuries of looking to the stars, scientists were now looking farther—and with more accuracy—into the heavens than ever before. Yet with all their scientific advances, there were still an infinite number of questions that remained unanswered. These were the questions that crowded her mind: questions that drove her to the study of quantum field theory, wave function, and the Schroedinger equation of particle mechanics...principles of relativity, Hubble's law, and Doppler shifts. Questions that ultimately circled back around to the one key issue: the origin and evolution of the physical universe, which seemingly appeared to have been created from nothing.

"...but more importantly, that's where you focused your undergraduate and postgrad studies," Ed was saying. "This man has asked for us to assign him an assistant. He specifically requested someone with an interest and background in the origins of the universe." Gillian's heart began to race as he spoke.

"You know, of course, that there are a number of current-day studies focusing on the first moments after the universe came into existence. So far, we can guess what happened as far back as 10^{-43} seconds after the universe began. The purpose of the study you'll be involved in is to go back even further in time—if it is even possible." Ed licked his lips, as if savoring the juicy project.

"You'll be collecting and analyzing data from other observers who have been working on similar theories. You may even serve as an observer, collecting necessary data—including photometric plots, spectral plates, and ccd images—at one of the major observatories. This will add to your workload, of course, but I'm sure you will agree that this opportunity is worth?..."

Gillian found her mind wandering as he rambled on about her good fortune. *I can't believe this!* She resisted the urge to hug her knees to her chest like a delighted child. *Finally, a project with some substance! Maybe I'll get to make suggestions, even contribute to the work as a whole....* The fact that she didn't know the full details of the assignment did not concern her. It was a full-fledged research project, and she'd be working directly under?...

Max.

Dr. Max Bishop, Ph.D., graduate cum laude from Harvard University, former student at Princeton, where Gillian's father had once been a distinguished professor. Former research astronomer at Rome Astronomical Observatory...and former heartthrob to the lovesick teenager Gillian had been.

The horrible truth rang in her mind like a death sentence. What was she thinking? She'd been so caught up in the excitement of getting a real assignment, she'd forgotten for a moment exactly who was in charge of the project. This was terrible! She couldn't work with *Max Bishop!* It had taken her years to make him a part of her past. She certainly didn't want him to become an integral part of her future....

Suddenly, she became aware that Ed was staring at her, apparently waiting for some sort of response.

"What was that?" she asked, feeling her cheeks turn warm.

"I'm sorry, Ed, I—"

The man blinked at her, then rolled his eyes heavenward, as if wondering at the wisdom of giving Gillian a key role in such an important project. "I asked if that would be a problem— going down to Palomar Observatory to make some observations in late August. Dr. Bishop may go with you, depending on how your work develops over the next month or so, but I suspect you'll be going alone."

Gillian just stared at him. *A trip to Palomar Observatory? At the university's expense? I must be hearing things....* "No, of course that will be fine." She heard herself speaking, as if in a daze.

"Of course," Ed said dryly. Gillian raised her head and gave him a questioning look, but his face betrayed nothing. Was he laughing at her? Did he suspect that she was hiding something? She couldn't tell. "Well, why don't we go introduce you to Dr. Bishop and get you started? Unless, of course, you were planning on getting yourself some lunch first?" Gillian hesitated. She had planned to finally approach Max this morning; Bridget's request had forced the issue. But now the prospect was not appealing in the least. She was still trying to figure out how to respond when she saw a shadow pass the office entrance. Ed turned in his chair, just as the figure disappeared from view.

"Wait a minute...I think that was him." He stood and stuck his head out in the hallway. "Wait up there...Max." Ed smiled as the person down the corridor apparently turned to face him. "Say, do you have a second? I'd like to introduce you to your new research assistant."

Gillian felt her body begin to tremble. *Okay, girl. Here we go. The moment you've been dreading. Try not to embarrass yourself.*

Just then, a tall, muscular figure filled the doorway. Gillian stared. Amazingly, unbelievably, there he stood. This man appeared much older than the youthful Max Bishop she had known. Gone was the youthful fervor, but in its place rested an aura of seasoned maturity. When she looked into his brilliant blue eyes, she knew he was the same gorgeous man she had dreamt of so long ago, only better.

Max opened his mouth, then snapped it shut again without speaking. For a moment, there was silence between him and Gillian, as there had been the day they first met. But this time, she could not find the words to fill the empty air. After several long moments, he was the first to speak.

"Is it possible? Can it be...*my* little Gilly Spencer?"

Gillian's heart leapt in her chest. Suddenly, it was as if time had not passed. She was a child again. And as if it were yesterday, every fiber of her being remembered how it felt to be his.

Three

Love won't be tampered with, love won't go away.
Push it to one side and it creeps to the other.
LOUISE ERDRICH, "THE RELIGIOUS WARS,"
THE BINGO PALACE, 1994

June 30, 1987

This morning, I awoke to the sound of a bird singing right outside my window. I suppose it would be more poetic to say "a lark" or "a robin," rather than just "a bird," but the truth is, I don't know anything about birds since I never paid much attention to them before. Is this a sign that I am, really and truly, falling in love?

Well, whatever was singing, I was all excited because I knew that Max was coming today. The last time he was here, I'd been wearing one of my scrungiest outfits—long cutoffs, beat-up old thongs, and a white T-shirt covered with dust from Mom's potatoes and a bit of brown juice from the potato peelings. I was Cinderella...straight out of the cinders.

This time, I made sure I looked my best. I didn't have a fairy god-mother who could transform me completely, but I did have Jenny. I called her first thing this morning, and she came right over to do something with my hair. The last perm I got sort of frizzed it out. The best Jenny could do was French braid it, but it helped a lot just to get it under control. After Jenny was done fixing my hair, I got her to pin it up in back so I didn't look like such a kid. Jenny called me "Swiss Miss" then, but I ignored her. I thought I looked pretty cool.

After Jenny left, I put on my favorite outfit: a pink-and-white jumper Mom bought for me last month. I saw it in a magazine and had to have it. I was a little bit disappointed once I tried it on, though. The model in the magazine filled it out a lot better than I did. But it was still cute, just right for a hot day like today.

Next, I chose my props. One of Mom's chaise lounges, my sunglasses, and a glass of lemonade. That would make me look cool, I thought. Finally, I decided to grab a book from my shelf. What could be more casual than reading in the backyard? I started to grab Northanger Abbey—I love Jane Austen's ridiculous heroine, Catherine—but then thought better of it. In the end, I picked up Dad's copy of The Odyssey. I didn't know anything about the story, but the title sounded pretty sophisticated, anyway.

I got everything set up by a quarter to eleven, and not a moment too soon, 'cause Max was early. I was reading page one of The Odyssey for the fifth time when he came into the yard.

"Hey, Max," I said, looking up and turning to the middle of the book. I tried to sound bored but that was hard to do with him standing in front of me, wearing a navy-colored Princeton sweatshirt that brought out the blue in his eyes.

"Hey, kiddo." He smiled back at me. I felt my heart do a little flip.

I looked down at my watch. "You're early," I told him.

"Am I?" Max sounded surprised. He casually tucked his hands into the back pockets of his jeans. "I was afraid I might be late. I've been walking around this morning, thinking, and I forgot my watch. I have a tendency to lose track of time."

More than anything, I wanted to ask him what he thought about when he walked. But that seemed kind of personal, and I was afraid he might tell me to mind my own business.

"Maybe I'll just sit down and talk with you for a few minutes then, if I'm early. You'll tell me when it's time to go in?" He looked around for someplace to sit, and I wanted to smack myself. How stupid could I be? I'd brought out only one chaise lounge. Now there wasn't anyplace for Max to sit. Of course, that meant he would go inside my Dad's office to wait.

But he didn't. He just looked around, then planted himself on the ground, right by my feet. He looked really cute, sitting there in the thick, green grass. For a minute, I imagined myself as some sort of Egyptian princess on top of my throne, with Max as my adoring slave. But the thought was so ridiculous, I had to bite my lip to keep from laughing.

"So, what do you think of our hero, Odysseus?" he asked me, looking at the book I held in my hands.

"I don't know," I said, then held my breath. That, at least, was an honest statement. I figured I sounded dumb, but Max nodded as if my comment had been truly profound.

"Good idea," he said. "Holding off your judgment until the end."

I never thought I could love anyone so much in my whole life. After that, I wasn't sure what to say. "Nice weather," maybe? Even I knew that was dumb. His studies with Dad seemed like my best bet.

"So...how do you like having my dad as your advisor?" I asked. I braced myself for the answer I knew had to be coming. Dad's students always went on and on about how great he was. I always thought it was pretty nauseating, especially since Dad never showed that side of himself to his own daughter. But Max surprised me.

"It's incredible, having this opportunity to get extra help in my studies. I want to do the best that I can in my field. This is important to me. Really important, Gilly," he said. "There's something about astronomy that I find really intriguing. I guess it's just that...everyday life is just so sterile, you know? So predictable. We get up in the morning, we go to school—or to work—we eat our breakfast, feed the dog...and act like that's all there is. We don't notice that all around us, there are other planets, other galaxies. We don't acknowledge that we're just a tiny part of this incredible universe...of a bigger plan. Most days, we don't even look up...."

41

I watched him as he spoke, and his eyes lit up with the same fire they'd had in them that day I saw him arguing with Dad.

"Dad doesn't believe there's a bigger plan," I said and took a drink of my lemonade.

Max stopped and looked at me. "I know," he said simply. "What do you think?"

I just blinked at him. I couldn't remember the last time anyone asked me what I thought. "Well, Mom says that there is a God, and that he's the one in control of the universe."

"I see," said Max. Then he repeated, "What do you think?"

I was quiet for a minute. I wasn't quite sure what to say. "I think I believe in God," I told him finally. "But I believe in science, too. I guess I don't think about it too much because I don't want to have to choose."

Max nodded seriously. "Exactly," he said.

I didn't get it. "Exactly…what?" I asked.

Max looked at me thoughtfully. "Has your dad ever mentioned his theory about all things being provable?" I shook my head. Normally, I would have been embarrassed or angry that one of Dad's students knew something about him that I didn't. But this wasn't just any student.

"Well," Max went on, "your father believes that there is a scientific explanation for everything…we scientists just have to find it."

Then he went on about how some ancient Greeks thought the earth was the center of the universe, and since they couldn't prove it, they made up a theory and believed it anyway. He was so intense that I let him go on—he's even cuter when he's really into something.

"Don't you see, Gilly?" he said. "It didn't make any sense!"

I just stared at him.

"You mean, because they thought the sun and the planets circled the earth?" I asked.

"Yes, but it's more than that," he insisted. "They needed a theory to explain why the planets didn't orbit in a perfect circle, so they made one up! They couldn't prove it; they just wanted to believe it. Eventually, though, we were able to prove that the planets travel around the sun. At first people felt threatened by this. The idea that the earth wasn't at the center of the universe challenged their assumptions about the relationship between God and man. But in time, it became clear that everything we've learned about the nature of the universe is consistent with Scripture—and with what we know of God."

Max's eyes got real intense after that. "See, those people had faith, but they didn't have the proof to back it up. But every day, we find more scientific evidence that supports a God-made universe." He looked at me real funny, as if just noticing that I was still there. "Gilly, your father believes that given enough time, man can prove anything that's scientifically true...and I agree with him."

"You do?" This surprised me.

"I do. And I'm going to do it, someday."

I was almost afraid to ask. "Going to do what?"

Max leaned forward intently, and I nearly fell off the chaise as I inched forward to hear what he was going to say. "I believe someone created the universe, Gilly. But I'm not going to just believe it. Someday, I'm going to prove it!"

As I looked into his bright eyes, I wondered if he could. Mom would have said, no, it wasn't possible, that God's ways aren't ours to know. But Mom has been hardened by years of fighting with Dad over science and religion. Could Max really do what he said he would? I couldn't help but wonder.

And even though I wasn't sure what I thought about God, myself, I couldn't help but hope that he would succeed.

June 14, 1997

Gillian blinked against the fluorescent lighting behind Max's head. For a moment, the room swam, and she found it hard to focus. Could she be imagining things? Was it really him? She blinked hard, clearing her vision, and looked again.

The years had made their mark on Max, that much was certain. But even in the unnatural light he was, indeed, "gorgeous," as Bridget had claimed. Drawing upon her years of scientific training, Gillian turned a careful, observer's eye on him.

Gone was the shaggy brown hair she had once loved and, in its place, a head of closely shorn locks. At one temple, a single, unruly curl poked out like a spring, effectively keeping him from looking *too* professional, yet making him appear even more endearing than when Gilly had first known him. His face was generally as she remembered it, albeit a little older. Tiny laugh lines tickled the corners of his eyes, although he was not laughing now. His skin looked tougher, hardly the same baby-soft skin she remembered from his college days. She knew he wasn't one to waste his time "catching rays." It couldn't be attributed to anything but age. She'd heard about Max's reputation as a prolific writer of scientific papers—it sounded like he worked all the time. Max had never struck her as being a workaholic, but she could see him getting caught up in the subject if it was close to his heart. *Maybe he does look older,* she admitted. *But, still, he wears his age well.* The thought came, unbidden.

The collegiate sweatshirts had been replaced—not by the mandatory white shirt and synthetic-weave slacks worn by most nerdy scientists, Gillian was relieved to see, but by a blue plaid chambray shirt and cream-colored khakis. She almost smiled. Working with Ed had made her almost believe in the scientist stereotype. It was nice to be reminded that some of her future peers had style. Bit by bit, she drank in every detail of his appearance, as if she were starved for it.

Suddenly, Gillian felt very aware of her own body. Her lungs were taking in short, shallow breaths, and she could almost feel the blood coursing warmly through her veins. Seeing Max again was having an even greater effect on her than she had expected it would. But how could she not feel *something* after seeing that compelling face again...that strong, tapered nose...that masculine chin?

It was Max's eyes, however, that tugged at her heart. Whenever she thought of him—and, although she hated to admit it, she still did from time to time—she remembered the flash those eyes had held. Some people wore their hearts on their sleeves; Gillian had always believed that Max wore his in his eyes. She looked at him intently, fighting the urge to turn away. Kindness and compassion were still there. So was his heart. And suddenly, her own heart seemed to be beating stronger than ever before.

Steadily, Max matched her gaze. For a moment, he did not speak—whether to give her time to finish her silent assessment, or because he couldn't think of anything to say, Gillian could not tell. Finally, he stepped toward her. Instinctively, nervously, she took a tiny step back. As if to help her catch her balance, Max reached forward and took her two trembling hands into his own.

"The years have been good to you, Gilly," he said quietly but with great feeling.

Gillian cleared her throat and forced a smile. "Always full of compliments, aren't you, Max?" she said, remembering the day they had first met, when he had told her she wore her age well. Then, afraid that her comment sounded barbed, she squeezed his hands enthusiastically before pulling away. Max narrowed his eyes a bit but said nothing.

"Well, here he is, Ed. The very famous *Dr.* Max Bishop!" she said brightly, emphasizing the word *doctor.* She decided it would be best to distance herself from Max as much as possible, although how she was going to do that after being assigned to his project was a question she was not yet prepared to answer.

"I take it you two know each other…uh, pretty well?"

At the look on Ed's face, Gillian had to laugh. Never at his best in social situations, her boss now looked like a trapped animal. Clearly, he did not know what to make of the situation or how he should respond. No doubt Ed thought that the two of them were former lovers or something. For heaven's sake. Nothing could be further from the truth. She might as well put that suspicion to rest, right away…and try to collect her dignity—what little dignity she had left where Max was concerned.

"Max was a student of my father's years ago," she said cheerfully, turning to Ed. From the corner of her eye, she could see Max looking at her, but she kept her full attention focused on her boss. "What has it been, Max? Eleven, twelve years?" Finally, she permitted herself a quick peek at him.

"Uh…ten, I believe." Max squinted at her curiously, as if trying to read her.

"Ten? Is that all?" She started to act surprised, then decided to abandon her attempt at pretense. "Well, that seems about right, I suppose. Anyway, Max was sort of the older brother I never had. And I suspect I was the little sister he never wanted!" She forced a laugh.

"Oh, I wouldn't say that," Max said in a low voice.

Gillian felt her palms beginning to sweat. "Oh, Max. That's sweet." She tried to meet his gaze but found that she quickly had to turn away. Those eyes…they still saw too much. She could tell.

"Anyway, Ed," she continued, "we haven't seen each other in years. This is—this is…" She fought for words. "Well, it's quite a shock!" That was certainly no exaggeration.

"Yes, it is," Max agreed, folding his arms across his chest. "Although, it really shouldn't be. I started out at Princeton, even though I later transferred; it's logical that I would come back

46

here someday to continue my research. And you...well, it makes sense that you would go to Princeton, too. I imagine your dad insisted."

"You'd better believe it." Gillian laughed, her first spontaneous laugh of the morning. She wiped her sweaty palms against her pant legs.

"Frankly, I'm surprised to find you in this department, though," he said, raising his eyebrows. "I never knew you were so interested in astrophysics."

"Well...let's just say it's an interest that developed in the years after I met you," Gillian said softly. "My father, and *you*," she admitted, "were so passionate about the subject, I finally decided to figure out for myself what it was all about." It was true. She had resisted her initial interest in astronomy until after Max had left the university and her mother and father had become separated. After those two events, Gillian's fragile trust in other human beings had been seriously undermined. Not knowing who might leave her next, she threw herself into her studies instead of relationships. After Max and her father had left, she clung to astronomy as one final connection to the two men she loved most. Eventually, she got over Max. But her love for the stars remained.

"And what did you discover?" Max asked, taking one step closer to her.

"I discovered...that I fell in love," Gillian answered softly, her mind focused on images from the past. In the silence that followed, she noticed Max's questioning look. "With astronomy!" she said quickly, then felt ridiculous about trying to explain. Of course he knew she was talking about her studies! Surely he never would have suspected how she once felt about him. She'd been nothing more than a child. It was nothing but a silly schoolgirl crush....

"Of course you did." Max smiled. "Who wouldn't?" Once

again, Gillian remembered how he had responded to her most embarrassing teenage moments, making them seem perfectly natural and putting her completely at ease. Max had always been kind. It was a relief to see that, in this respect at least, he had not changed.

He reached forward and grabbed her clammy hands once again, drawing her arms up in the air at her sides, and bathing her in the warmth of his grin. "Just look at you, Gilly!" he said, employing the childhood name no one else used anymore. "You're all grown up!" His eyes took in the tailored lilac linen shirt, the fitted white slacks, the slim white sandals on her feet. Then his gaze flickered upward to her lightly made-up face, her honey-colored mane, which she had parted down the middle that morning before pulling together in the pencil-twist knot. Finally, Max's eyes came to rest upon her own hazel ones. Sometimes when she was excited, Gillian knew, her eyes had golden flecks in them. Surely those flecks were there now. Did Max notice them?

Suddenly, the absurdity of the thought struck her. What did it matter if Max appreciated her eyes? She had a boyfriend, for goodness sake. She was dating a *very nice man.* A man who cared about her. One who wasn't going to leave her. She had been down this road before with Max...thinking about him, dreaming about him, for years after he was gone. She knew what it was like *not* to be loved by Maxwell Bishop. She didn't need to revisit those feelings. Perhaps it wasn't the most comfortable situation in the world, but she would find a way to work with Max without mooning about him or getting too attached to him. He was her new supervisor...nothing more. This was no time to get emotionally involved. *You don't need him, Gilly,* she told herself. *You've been over him for a long time now, remember? This is shock you're feeling, nothing more....*

"Yep, I'm all grown up." Gillian spoke cheerfully. "I'm a scientist now, just like you." She pulled away from his gentle grip.

"Married?" Max asked casually.

Gillian swallowed hard against the lump in her throat. "No, but I might as well be! I've been seeing someone for quite a while. We're very happy," she said through stiff lips. "So you see, I *am* all grown up now. I guess I'm not the same little girl you remember," she told Max firmly, more for her own benefit than for his.

"I guess not." Max sounded vaguely disappointed, but Gilly guessed that was due to her coolly composed response, and not the fact that she was seeing someone. She knew that Max had always been fond of her. "Brotherly" was an accurate description of how he had felt toward Gillian, she was sure. Perhaps he expected a more enthusiastic welcome? A hug maybe? An "It's good to see you"? Or at the very least, sustained eye contact?

The thought made Gillian feel terrible. Why couldn't she greet Max graciously? He had been nothing but kind to her, as long as she had known him. It wasn't his fault that as a child she had fallen in love with him, only to be left behind. But she couldn't do it. She could not give away too much of herself. His presence alone was disturbing enough. If she looked into his eyes for long, he would see how his unexpected appearance had shaken her. He would know how deeply, how dearly, he had been missed.

"Won't Dad be surprised to hear that I saw you!" she said brightly, keeping a cheerful smile plastered on her face.

"How is your father these days?" Max asked evenly. He continued to watch her every move.

"Oh, he's doing…pretty well," Gillian answered slowly. It was hard to respond, with her mouth feeling like cotton. "He moved down to Florida after he retired. Mom moved to D.C. Dad's there now, though, visiting her."

"Your folks split up?" Max didn't look surprised. "I'm so

sorry. That…that must have been awful for you. And for them."

Gillian nodded. "Yeah, well, a lot of people had been expecting it. Mom and Dad separated for the first time, actually, the year after you left."

This last bit caught him off guard. "I had no idea they were having that much trouble," Max told her, shaking his head. "I'm sorry," he said again, then looked embarrassed that he had repeated himself.

"They've kept in contact, though, over the years. The divorce was never actually finalized. They have most of the same problems they always did, but they're still trying to work things out. That's something…."

"Good for them." Max looked like he wanted to say something, then shut his mouth, as if he could find no further words to offer. It was sad, Gillian thought. They'd never run out of things to say to each other before. But that was a lifetime ago.

"A-*hem*," Ed cleared his throat, and Gillian blushed, having forgotten he was even in the room. Certainly the conversation had pushed the limits of what the socially challenged man could handle.

"Sorry, Ed." She grinned. "Guess you just got a little more information about me and my family than you needed, huh?"

Just then a petite figure appeared in the doorway behind Max, and Gillian heard Bridget's singsong voice ring out. "Hey, Gillian!" she said. "There you are! I've been looking everywhere for you! I thought maybe we could go to—oh, hello!" She smiled brightly, flashing her big brown eyes at Max, then nodding politely at Ed. "I'm Gillian's roommate, Bridget Atwood. She and I were going to grab a bit to eat. Would you two like to join us?"

Gillian blinked. *Whoa. That girl doesn't waste any time.*

Max shook the hand Bridget offered and smiled. "Certainly. I'd be delighted."

"Not me." Ed looked like a cornered animal ready to bolt. "But by all means, you three go. In fact," he glanced at his watch, "you'd better hurry if you don't want to get stuck in the noon rush."

Poor Ed, Gillian thought. *He knows it's too late for that. He just wants to get his office back.* Taking her cue from Ed, she slipped past Max and worked her way to the door. As she passed, Bridget gave her a conspiratorial smile. Gillian's heart sank. Suddenly the prospect of spending the next hour watching her roommate flirt with Max was more than she could take.

"I'm afraid I'm going to have to bow out, too," she said quickly, trying to sound full of regret. "My computer crashed this morning, and I'm going to have to redo those calculations before I start working on your project," she told Max. "But why don't you two go ahead?"

Max looked confused. Bridget was delighted. Gillian just felt nauseous. But Bridget seized the opening like a seasoned professional, chatting animatedly with Max, slipping one hand casually into the crook of his arm, and leading him out the door toward the university cafeteria.

Gillian watched them go. *Kind of like a lamb to the slaughter,* she thought, cynically. *That poor guy hasn't got a chance.* But despite herself, Gillian couldn't ignore the thought: *If Max is the victim here, how come I'm the one who feels like crying?*

Four

July 7, 1987

What a terrible thing it is to love someone! Why is it that people say love is wonderful? It's not wonderful at all. It stinks, if you ask me. I'd say that I'd rather have both ears cut off, but that's not really true. I don't want to lose my ears. But I don't want to lose Max, either...not that he was ever mine. Now it looks like he never will be.

All right, let me back up and explain. The trouble started this morning, when Dad called home to say that he had left a big important folder on the desk in his office, and would Mom please come bring it to him? The thing was, Mom had a big important phone call of her own scheduled for noon, and she couldn't leave the house. Instead, she asked Norrie to drive me, so I could take the papers to him.

I didn't mind. I've always liked going to the university. During the school year, it's always full of students rushing off to someplace important—a class or a date, I suppose, and it's so beautiful in the summer, when there are fewer people around to tear up the grass. When I was little, Mom would take me with her to visit Dad, and I would pretend that we were on the grounds of our very own castle. It doesn't especially look like a castle to me anymore, but it did at the time. What can I say? I was a kid.

These days, I like to pretend that I'm one of the students. When I was younger, it was a crazy idea. But now that I'm getting older, it's not so farfetched. I don't get as many people looking at me, like they're thinking, "What are you doing here?" This morning, I figured I'd play "student" again, so I told Norrie she could stay in the car. She didn't mind this, either. It's quite a walk to Dad's office, and if you know Norrie, you'll remember that she isn't exactly a big fan of walking.

So, I grabbed the papers from the front seat, told Norrie I'd be right back, and headed off to the Physics Department. By now it may have occurred to you that there was a possibility of me running into a certain someone. Well, believe me, the thought had crossed my mind, too. I tried to act pretty casual as I looked around the campus. I was almost to the physics building, and just about to give up, when I finally saw him.

There he was: Max Bishop. It felt a bit strange to see him someplace other than my house. I had come to think of him as being my own special property. Usually, I try not to think too much about where he goes when he leaves our house. And I only think about his time with Dad as it relates to developing my understanding of Max's passion for astronomy. But here was the proof. Sure enough, Max exists outside of my world. He has another life. He has his classes….

He has a girlfriend.

I guess I always knew this was a possibility. But seeing for myself that it's true…well, that hit me harder than I thought it would.

The thing is, I'm not as deluded as I sound. I know I'm sixteen years old, and Max is, like, what? Twenty-three? It's not that I expect him to love me now. I just wish, somehow, that he could, you know…wait. He couldn't ever find someone who would love him as much as I do. I don't think that's scientifically possible. I liked him at first because he's cute. But once I got to know him, I realized that Max is so much more. He's kind and intelligent and passionate about what he believes in. He's really sweet to me...much nicer than any of the kids at my school. And he pays more attention to me than my parents ever do. How could I not love him?

But there he was, sitting on a bench next to a girl with long, dark hair and eyes the color of violets. I've read that description in books before, and I thought it was made up. Who on earth has eyes the color of violets? But this girl did. Technically, they were kind of blue, like the dark African kind. But they were like violets, just the same.

I'm not sure how long I stood there, watching them, but it felt like forever. Finally, I opened up Dad's folder, stuck my nose inside, and strolled casually over to where they were at, stopping behind them, just a few feet from where they were sitting. I heard Max's voice first.

"Of course I want to see you tonight, Angela," he was saying. "But I have to study. You know that."

The girl did not look happy, but she batted her eyelashes at him anyway. It looked kind of scary, from where I was at.

"Come on, Max. You know that's not true," she said. "You study every night. You don't have to tonight. You just want to. Admit it: you'd rather study than be with me."

I couldn't believe she was saying this...to Max! I've heard of emotional manipulation before, I'd just never seen it in action. My folks aren't so shy; when they're mad at each other, they just come right out and say so. I don't like it that they fight, but at least they fight fair.

I peeked over my folder at Max. Was he going to crumble? It sure looked like he might. Angela had him trapped in her tractor beam. I think he was hypnotized by those eyes. He laid one hand on Angela's bare arm and squeezed it, while leaning over to whisper something into her ear. My stomach flopped. I wanted to squeeze my eyes shut and just disappear. At the very least, I wanted to sneak away. But for some reason, my legs just wouldn't move. I waited to see what the girl was going to do.

Apparently she was waiting to see what she'd do next, too,

because for a minute she didn't say a word. She was looking pretty confused. I guess her temper tantrum wasn't getting her the response she was expecting.

"Are you saying that you won't come over to Vicky's with me tonight?" she pouted. What a trooper. She must have thought it was worth one more try.

"Now, Angela. You know you'll have a great time at Vicky's whether I'm there or not. Half the time you girls just go into a corner and talk about us guys, anyway. Why don't you just do that and pretend that I'm there?"

That last bit kind of surprised me. It almost sounded like Max was making fun of her, and that's not like him at all. Maybe he was just getting frustrated. I could see why he would, if that's the kind of pressure he got from Angelllaaaaaa. Yuk.

Well, Angela wasn't buying it. "I don't think so, Max. You're going to have to do better than that if you want people to think you care about me. How would it look if I showed up by myself?"

"Angela." Max looked pretty serious now. "That's the point. I don't care what other people think. I care what you and I think. Don't you know that you're important to me? Don't you know how much you—"

My lunch started to come back for a visit. It was time to go, I couldn't listen to any more. Out of some sort of primitive survival instinct, my feet finally started moving. Somehow, they carried me to my dad's office, even though I wasn't really paying attention to where I was going. Dad was kind of grumpy, I guess because it took me so long to get him his precious folder. But once it was in his hands, he was fine again.

Wish I could say the same thing about me.

June 14, 1997

From her position on the back section of the wraparound porch, Gillian could just make out Cassiopeia's "W" twinkling over the stand of her neighbor's hawthorn trees. Lifting her eyes upward, she quickly picked Ursa Major out of the night sky, then directly overhead, tucked between Boötes the Herdsman and Hercules, she found one of her favorite constellations: the Corona Borealis or, as she had known it as a child, the Northern Crown. Seeing it was like coming upon an old friend.

Gillian drew in a deep breath of fresh, clean country air, wrapped both arms around herself, and sighed deeply. She loved living in Princeton again. It had been easy for her father to convince her that Princeton was the best school. After being dragged off to Washington, D.C., following her parents' initial separation, she had constantly dreamed about coming back. Scenes from her childhood home had haunted her: beautiful Battlefield Park, the towpath leading along Canal Road and the Delaware-Raritan Canal, the marshy remains of what was once Lake Passaic but was now the Great Swamp, the boardwalk at Atlantic City.

The city had made her claustrophobic and homesick, too, for the company of the wildlife she had grown to love: the wood ducks and bitterns, the deer and fox and field mice...even the fireflies. *Especially* the fireflies. How was it possible that when people from out of state thought of New Jersey, their thoughts immediately turned to oil refineries and the turnpike, and not the beautiful landscape that had given the Garden State its name? The logic escaped her. People could joke all they wanted about living in *"Joisey,"* but Gillian knew in her heart that it would always be her home.

The old white farmhouse she now lived in was a dream come true as well. After her folks split up, her mom had dragged her from one condo to the next. For years Gilly had dreamed of setting down roots once again. Finally, during her first year of undergrad work at the university, she had moved into this place, which she could truly call home. She'd had several roommates since. So far, Bridget had lasted the longest: eight months, Pam just a little less at six. It was a comfortable enough arrangement. The women all liked one another and joked around quite a bit, though it was clear that each had her own life. It made things easier, there was much less to argue about. Gillian wanted to keep it that way.

With deft movements, she reached down and quickly removed the eyepiece from the telescope she had dragged out of the attic that afternoon, replacing it with one of a higher magnification. In her hand, the first piece felt familiar and comforting. It had been years since she'd used this old 'scope. It was useless in her university studies and horribly outdated, even for amateur use. She had several other telescopes, all of them more powerful and expensive, but this particular refractor had always been her favorite.

She was still messing with the eyepiece when Bridget bounded out onto the porch.

"Gillian Spencer," she cried breathlessly. "You are the *best* roommate in the whole world!" With a happy flounce, she threw herself against the cushions of the porch swing.

"Oh, really?" Gillian tried to sound nonchalant as she finished setting up her telescope.

"Yes, *really!* Taking off like that and leaving me with that guy, Max. *Veeeeery* nice," she said appreciatively. "I thought you didn't know who he was, by the way. He sure seemed to know a lot about *you*."

"He did?" Gillian's head popped up, as if of its own accord. "Like what?"

"Oh, he knew about your dad, where you lived when you were a kid. Stuff like that."

"Right." Gillian turned back to the 'scope. "He was one of my dad's students."

"That's what he said." Bridget looked at her curiously. "Is something the matter, Gil?"

"No," Gillian said stiffly. "Not at all. Why do you ask?"

"No reason." Bridget shrugged. "Your voice just sounded a little strained." She settled back against her pillows, her concern about Gillian's mood quickly forgotten. "Anyway, I *have* to tell you all about lunch!"

"Do you really?" Gillian mumbled, but quietly so Bridget could not hear her.

Over the next twenty minutes, Gillian was subjected to a running commentary on the details of Bridget's lunch date, including: "Max ordered broccoli at the cafeteria. Can you believe it? Everybody knows better than that!" and, "I know he's a real gentleman, because he didn't ask, 'Are you going to eat that?' and take the leftover food off my plate when I was done." By the time her friend had finally paused to catch her breath, Gillian knew that Max had been in Princeton for nine days, that he had spent the last three years conducting research at an observatory in Rome, and that he had shown more than a passing interest in her relationship with Keith Waterford.

"What did he find so intriguing about my love life?" she mumbled crossly. "I haven't seen the guy in ten years. What business is it of his *who* I date?"

Bridget lifted her shoulders in an almost imperceptible shrug. "I dunno. He just asked what the guy was like, was he good to you, did you love him. You know, stuff like that."

"Well, what did you tell him?" Gillian asked, more sharply than she intended.

Bridget sat up straight and looked at Gillian intently. "What do you think I told him? I told him you were extremely happy. You *are* extremely happy. *Aren't* you?"

"Of course I am."

"Are you sure?"

"Yes, I'm happy. You know I am. Happy, happy, happy."

"Well, you sure don't look it." Bridget stared at her, then asked, "What's going on?"

"It's nothing, Bridget. I—"

"Gillian…"

"I said it's nothing. Really!"

"But—"

"Bridget, *stop* it! Just back off!" She practically spat out the words. Bridget's brown eyes opened wide and began to glisten. She stared at Gillian wordlessly. "Oh, Bridget." Gillian sighed. "I'm sorry. I didn't mean that. I just…" her voice trailed off. She wished her friend would break in and say, "It's okay. You don't have to explain." But no such offer came.

She tried again. "Look, it's just that…well, Max's coming here brought up a lot of old stuff from my childhood, that's all."

Bridget sniffed. "You mean stuff about your parents?" she asked quietly. It was one of the few details of Gillian's personal life that she shared with her roommates. It was pretty much unavoidable. After several months of living together, most roommates eventually asked why her parents rarely called. Gillian usually explained that she didn't have a close relationship with her folks…and left it at that.

"Well…sort of. But it's more than that. It's—" She stopped, wondering how much she should explain. It wasn't that she didn't trust Bridget to understand her feelings. It was just that Bridget was already emotionally involved as well. Gillian had seen this situation many times in school. It was always difficult when two friends liked the same man, even if one of the crushes was completely in the past—as Gillian's was. She just wanted to handle the situation carefully.

"Do you remember when I told you about a guy I liked when I was a kid?" She seemed to recall a conversation they'd had a while back, in which Bridget had pressured her to explain why she never gave the men she dated a decent chance. Gillian had mumbled something vague about getting burned as a teenager.

Bridget thought for a moment. "It seems like you said there was someone you had a crush on for a long time, but you didn't really go into it."

"Well..." Gillian paused. There really wasn't any easy way to say it. "The thing is, the guy was...Max."

Bridget's jaw dropped. "Stop it. You're kidding me."

Gillian shook her head. "I wish I were."

"So you're saying that you and Max..."

"No. I'm not saying anything about 'me and Max.' It was just me. A one-way crush. Unrequited love." She tried to make it sound melodramatic and funny. But to her own ears, it just sounded pathetic.

"Oh, Gil!" Bridget hopped down off the swing and tried to wrap her arms around her. "How awful! You must have felt—"

"Now, Bridget." Gillian gently untangled herself from her roommate's embrace. "I was just kidding. It wasn't as bad as all that," she protested, even though she knew in her heart that it *was*. "He wasn't my first boyfriend or anything. He was much, much older. A student of my father's. I was just a kid."

"But still—"

"'But' nothing. It's fine. *I'm* fine." She didn't want anyone's sympathy, least of all Bridget's. Gillian wasn't comfortable letting anyone too close. The last thing she needed was for her roommate to start prying into old feelings from her past, feelings that died long ago.

Bridget looked completely unconvinced. "It's just so *sad.*"

"No, it's not." Gillian shook her head firmly. She was starting to get irritated now. "Please, Bridget. Can we just drop it? It happened a long time ago. It brought a lot of memories back for me, seeing Max today. But I've dealt with them, and I'm fine."

"Well…" The wheels were turning in Bridget's head. "Of course you don't want me to see him again. That would be terrible for you."

"I never said that." Gillian swallowed hard, wondering what Bridget meant by "seeing him again."

"But, Gil, we're roommates! You're obviously heartbroken. I can't just—"

"Bridget!" Gillian scowled at her. "I am not 'obviously' *anything*. Could you please stop acting like I'm some kind of precious doll? I'm not going to break—especially over a *man*. And certainly not over a crush I had ten years ago. I went on with my life, remember? For crying out loud, I was just a *kid*. It didn't mean a thing." *Keep telling yourself that,* whispered a tiny voice inside her head. *Maybe one of these days you'll believe it.*

"Does Keith know?" Bridget whispered, as if sharing in a terrible secret.

"Does Keith know *what?*" Now she was really angry. "Bridget, there's nothing going on between Max and me…and *there never was*. Do you understand? Nothing. Nada. Zip. Zilch. A big, fat *nothing.*" With each word, she made a dramatic karate chop in the air with one hand.

"Gosh, Gillian. You don't have to get so upset." Bridget folded her arms protectively across her chest and sat back down on the swing. "I just don't want my dating Max to come between us."

Gillian's heart sank, but she tried to keep her face expressionless. "So…he asked you out, then?" She tried to adjust the eyepiece on her telescope, but her hands were shaking so badly she had to give up and slip them into her pockets. *Stop it, Gil. You're acting like a child again.*

"He said something about going out for coffee together

sometime next week," Bridget told her confidently. "I told him he could call me, and he said he would."

"Oh." Gillian sounded relieved, in spite of herself. "Is that all?" As soon as the words were out of her mouth, she knew she had made a terrible error in judgment.

"What do you mean, 'Is that all?'" Bridget bit her lower lip and looked at Gillian, pain clearly visible in her wide brown eyes.

You idiot, Gillian berated herself. *You know she's sensitive. You should have been more careful.* "Oh, Bridget, I'm sorry," she began, reaching out to touch her roommate's sleeve. "I shouldn't have—"

"No!" Bridget interrupted, pulling away sharply. "That's right, you *shouldn't* have. I was trying to be nice, Gillian. I don't care if you *did* like him once. That's no reason to act like he couldn't ever like *me.*"

"You're right, it's not. I didn't mean it like that." Gillian suspected that she should stop right there and almost did. But then, she could not resist offering one last bit of advice. "It's just that…well, I don't want you to get your hopes up. To get too attached. I've seen him with girls before," she said, remembering Angela…and herself. "I know what he's like."

"Oh?" Bridget said suspiciously. "What do you mean?"

"I mean…" Gillian looked deep into her friend's eyes, willing her to understand. "Oh, don't take this wrong. Max is a *really* nice guy, and he doesn't mean any harm. It's just that he has a way of…of…well, of making girls like him more than he likes them."

Bridget pulled back and stared at Gillian as if her hair had turned to snakes. "I can't believe you'd say that to me!" She sounded horrified.

Uh-oh. Gillian knew she had gone too far. "I don't mean that he doesn't like *you.* Wait! Please, listen—"

Bridget jumped down from the swing and ran toward the house, ignoring Gillian's apologies. After reaching out and grabbing the screen door violently with one hand, she turned and called back over one shoulder, "I'm sorry it's so hard for you to believe that Max might like me, Gillian. But I think he does. And I'm sorry, too, if it hurts your feelings, but I *am* going to go out with him—even if you don't believe he likes me enough to ask." With that, she flounced back inside, letting the wood door slam shut behind her.

For several moments, Gillian remained motionless, staring at the spot where her roommate had last stood. How on earth had this happened? The events of the last day seemed like a hazy dream—or, more accurately, a convoluted nightmare.

Finally, she tore her gaze away from the door and plopped herself down on the vacated porch swing. Above her head, the same stars that had comforted her as a child now shone down upon her like great winking eyes.

"I didn't mean it like it sounded," she grumbled. But there was no one there to listen, as usual. If only Keith were here. Normally, she liked the fact that she and Keith led such independent lives. But lately, he hadn't been around much. And even though she didn't feel entirely close to him, having a boyfriend somehow gave her the illusion of feeling connected to *someone*. If he was around, he would tell her that she hadn't done anything to deserve Bridget's wrath. He would support her. If she told him she was having a bad day, he would take her out to dinner, make witty conversation, help take her mind off her troubles.

Gillian found herself looking forward to his return. Things would get back to normal once Keith was home. And that would be happening soon. The thought pleased her. That was it. All she needed was Keith. That was the missing piece. Once he was back, she was sure, everything would be fine.

But that night, as she waited for sleep to overtake her, Gillian's last thoughts were not of her successful lawyer-boyfriend, but of an endearing scientist named Max.

Five

I flee who chases me, and chase who flees me.
OVID, THE LOVES, C. A.D. 88

July 9, 1987

Well, it's official. The "love bug" has struck Princeton. It turns out that Jenny's older sister, Marta, got engaged on the Fourth of July. I think Marta saw it coming, 'cause she's already got her bridesmaids' dresses picked out, and it's only been eight days. I went over to Jenny's house yesterday, and her mother was laying out the pattern. They're hideous: long, Pepto-Bismol pink prom dresses with wine-colored dingle-balls. Jenny even has to wear a pink hairnet with a velvet bow on top. Marta says it's old-fashioned, but I say it's dorky. I think she just wants to make sure she's the prettiest one there.

Sometimes I wonder if I'm ever going to get married. I've always dreamed that I would. I've always wanted to be special to someone, I mean really special, but I never really pictured myself with anyone specific before. If Max asked me, though, I know I'd say yes—after I was older, of course. But I'm not holding my breath. Angela seems to have her claws into him pretty deep.

Angela and Marta aren't the only ones in love. Jenny's been talking about Matt Ross an awful lot lately. He was in her Language Arts class last year, and she's fallen pretty hard. His cousin Chris moved to Princeton last spring, and Jenny thinks he and I would make a cute couple. I don't really know him, he's a whole year older than me. But Jenny said that Matt said that Chris thinks I'm cute. I don't know what I'd do if he asked me to go with him. I mean, I like Max, whether he wants me to or not. But I know I can't wait around for him forever. That's dumb. Mom says I'm too young to go on dates anyway, so I guess it doesn't really matter who wants to go out with me.

The other day, while I was over at Jenny's, Marta came home and was blabbing on and on about her boyfriend, Todd. I asked her what was so special about him. You know, what made her pick him for her husband, out of all those other goofy guys she's dated? It was so weird.... She got this funny little look on her face, like no one had ever asked her that before. Finally, she said, "I guess it's that he loves me, and that he's mine."

Jenny and I just looked at each other, but later we talked about how lame that was. There is no way I'd marry someone just because he wanted to be mine. Ick. Then I started thinking about what I did want in a husband, and I realized I'd never really thought about it before. That's why I've decided to make a list...so I know my future husband when I see him. So, here it is:

THINGS I WANT IN A HUSBAND—NON-NEGOTIABLE (Mom and I talked about boys before, and she says it's important to know the difference between negotiable and non-negotiable qualities): intelligent, sweet to me, fun to be with, does well in school, a successful job after we graduate ('cause I plan to have one, too), mature (no spitballs or food fights), nice to kids, and attractive. He and I should also believe the same things about God. My parents argue about that an awful lot. I don't want to be like that when I get married. I suppose that means I should figure out what I think one of these days.

THINGS I WANT IN A HUSBAND—NEGOTIABLE (because I'm mature enough to know that I can't have everything I want): good fashion sense. That's something I can fix. Hey, I never said I was willing to give up a lot.

It's sort of fun to write these things down and think about what it would be like to find someone like that. I have a hard time believing it'll ever happen, though. The guys at school aren't anything like...well, they're not anything like Max, who is exactly what I want. This is depressing. What good does it do me to know what I want when I'm never going to get it?

Mom says not to worry about boys, that I've got plenty of time for that. By the time I'm ready to get married, she says, most of the guys I know will be more mature, and I will have met dozens of others besides. I think she meant that to be comforting, but it makes me feel even worse. I'm not real excited about meeting dozens of geeky guys before I find one that's worth keeping. Maybe Mom's right. Maybe I won't be ready for love for a while. It's just hard, seeing Max with that girl, knowing that he's not waiting for me. I wish I was older. I wish I was the kind of girl he wanted to be with. I just wish things were different, but they're not, and I can't do anything about it!

I don't want to settle for anyone less than Max. Why doesn't he want to wait for someone who cares about him as much as I do?

June 18, 1997

"Happy birthday to me, happy birthday to *meeeeeee*." Gillian punched haphazardly at the keyboard of her computer. So far, it had been one of the worst birthdays on record...and she'd had some real whoppers. This year, she had been completely alone: Keith wouldn't be back until later that night, precluding any chance for a real celebration. Four days after her fight with Bridget, her roommate still wasn't speaking to her. Though Pam had left a gift-wrapped bottle of Gillian's favorite perfume outside her bedroom door that morning, she, too, had been making herself scarce all week—no doubt in an effort to keep herself out of the fray. And, as if things weren't bad enough, Gillian had been working double overtime to get caught up on Max's research.

"Phooey." She blinked at the numbers that danced in front of her eyes. Wearily, she slipped a pair of reading glasses from her head and laid them on the Formica desktop. Then, rubbing one hand absently against her brow, she glanced around the sterile-looking, but functional room. Oh, well. Things could be worse: she could still be at her temporary workstation. Though working with Max *did* present a whole new set of problems, the situation fortunately had its perks as well. Desks in the physics department were available on a first-come, first-served basis. Grad students often had to jockey for work space; from day to day, she had never known where she would be stuck. That was all over, thanks to Max's high-profile project—Ed had managed to snag them two tiny offices in a little-used hallway adjacent to the chem lab.

Gillian consulted the clock on the wall. Seven-fourteen. Keith's flight wasn't scheduled to arrive until 9:50. There wasn't any point in leaving now. Still, she figured, she wasn't going to make any progress if she didn't give her brain some kind of boost. She'd been dragging for the last two hours. Normally, she tried to keep apples or oranges or carrots sticks around. But her mind was so scattered today, she'd left her healthy snacks at home. As a result, she was starving and craving sugar...of *any* kind. The more empty and refined, the better.

She was hunched over her purse, desperately digging for loose change to feed the vending machine, when Max walked in.

"Hey, there." He raised one lanky arm in greeting. "Working kind of late, aren't you?"

Gillian bolted upright at the sound of his voice. "Umm. Yeah." She smiled stiffly. "My supervisor is quite a taskmaster." Max met her smile with his own, then looked awkwardly away. She drew in a deep breath. It was still difficult to relax around him. After four days, Max had picked up on her tension and

70

seemed to feel uncomfortable as well. Thankfully, he had his own office and had so far left her pretty much to herself.

"Are you starting to get up to speed on the work we've been doing in Rome?" he asked, flipping through a stack of notebooks piled near the door.

"Yeah. No problem." She nodded enthusiastically. Not only was the research project intriguing, it was *challenging*, which was a pleasant change. Gillian opened her mouth to ask about one particular calculation that had caught her attention, then thought better of it. She and Max would have plenty of opportunities to talk about his findings. Right now, it was late, and with any luck he would leave quickly. She just didn't have the emotional energy to deal with him. Not tonight.

But Max didn't leave. He just stood in the doorway, giving her a funny look.

"What's the matter?" she asked, feeling suddenly self-conscious. She ran down a mental checklist: Had she forgotten to comb her hair at some point in the day? Was she wearing two different-colored socks? Had something happened to her at dinner? "Oh no!" Her hand flew to her mouth. "There's a piece of lettuce stuck in my teeth, isn't there?"

Max looked taken aback, then his face broke into a wide grin and he began to laugh—a deep, rumbling chuckle that gave Gillian wonderful little chills. "No, no. Nothing like that," he assured her with a sly twist of his lips.

"Then what? What are you looking at?"

"Just...you."

"Why? What about me?" Her cheeks were burning up.

"Nothing. It's just that you're..."

"*Max...*" She couldn't believe her ears. Was he actually flirting with her?

"—you know, the birthday girl." He grinned again.

"*What?*" Gillian's face fell. She stared at him, dumbfounded.

Max might as well have called her the next Nobel Prize winner. "What are you talking about?"

He just smirked.

"How could you possibly know it's my birthday?"

He looked quite pleased with himself. "Well...I was thinking a little while ago about how strange, and...well, how *nice* it is, seeing you after all these years. My mind started filling up with all the memories of that summer—including the day I met you, when you told me that you had just turned seventeen."

Gillian felt her cheeks grow hot. "Now, that was a long time ago!" she protested. "You're not going to hold me responsible for what I said as a kid?" The look Max gave her was one of compassion and understanding, and she smiled back at him despite her best intentions not to.

"Of course not. I never held it against you back then, either. I knew you were trying to sound grown-up. Besides, I got you to 'fess up." He grinned. "But that memory made me realize your birthday had to be coming up. I ran up to Ed's office just now. He was still there, so I had him check your student file."

"You did?" Gillian didn't know what else to say. It seemed like a lot of effort for something that shouldn't have mattered to Max at all.

"I did. And I'm lucky, too. If this hadn't hit me until tomorrow, I'd have missed your birthday completely."

"Oh, that's okay." Dismissively, Gillian waved one hand in the air. Things were getting too personal. It was time to put an end to this conversation. She turned away and stashed her purse back under the desk. "You wouldn't be the first one."

"No?" Max looked at her closely. "Well...just the same, I'm glad I didn't. 'Cause then I wouldn't have been able to give you these." He reached into his coat pocket and pulled out two cream-filled, chocolate cupcakes, sealed in plastic.

"Junk food!" Gillian exclaimed happily, then jumped up to

accept the offered treat. "Where'd these come from?"

"The vending machine, of course. It's the best I could do on such short notice," Max explained. As he placed the package in her hands, his fingers gently brushed against hers. The feeling, warm and gentle, sent a wave of shock through her. For a moment, time remained frozen. The cupcakes blurred before her eyes. It had been a long time since anyone had put any effort into making her birthday special. Gillian smiled as a glimmer of a tear threatened to betray her true feelings. She quickly composed herself. "I'm afraid I don't have any candles," Max said, kindly covering for her emotional reaction. "But you can make a wish anyway, if you want."

Something about the offer made Gillian's stomach muscles constrict. "Uh...no, that's okay." She pulled her hands away and quickly wiped her eyes. What could she wish for in front of Max? This was becoming entirely too intimate.

"Are you sure?" Max sounded doubtful. Gillian looked up into his eyes and glimpsed a flicker of sadness in them. He was trying to be kind, and she was giving him the brush off. Again.

She gave him a tiny smile. "I don't need to make a wish, Max. I already got what I wanted."

"You did?" He tilted his head to one side.

"My wish was answered when I got assigned to this research project," she said gratefully. "I've been Ed's clerical slave for the past year, just *dying* to get my hands on some real work! Especially something like this. The data in these files is extraordinary, Max. It looks like you're doing what you've always wanted to do."

"Really?" Max looked at her, question written in his eyes. "And what have I always wanted to do?"

"Explore the origins of the universe."

Max grinned. "That's right. I'd forgotten that I told you about that."

"So have you done it yet?"

"Done what?"

"Proven that the universe was created by God?"

Max shook his head. "No. I'm afraid it isn't that easy. I had pretty lofty expectations for myself when I was a grad student. I'm not certain that we can *definitively* prove God as Creator. But every day, I am more convinced that scientific evidence points to him."

Gillian regarded him with a serious gaze. "That's what this study is about."

"It is." His eyes searched hers.

"Well, I'm not sure if I share your opinion yet," Gillian admitted. "But I'll admit, I *am* intrigued. And I'm looking forward to assisting you."

Max acknowledged her comments with a nod, then turned back toward the door. Before he left, he turned and gave her a final, searching look. "I appreciate your help, Gilly," he said simply. "It's good to be working with you...as a peer. And to finally *know* you as one."

Gillian sat motionless in her chair, trying not to read a deeper meaning into his words.

"And now, I hope you're going home soon. You must have some kind of birthday celebration planned."

"Mmhmm." She nodded. "Keith's coming home from his legal conference tonight. I'm picking him up at the airport."

"Well, then," Max said seriously. "I guess the research project isn't the only wish that came true for you this week, is it?"

Gillian opened her mouth to speak. But before she could answer, he was gone.

Gillian arrived at the airport, nervous, flustered, and nearly ten minutes late. Well, isn't this a fine welcome home! What on earth is Keith going to think? She'd been so engrossed in her reading, she hadn't even noticed the time. I'll just have to make it up to him, somehow.

When she reached the gate, however, the waiting area was still filled to overflowing with people who had come out to meet their loved ones. Gillian glanced at the airline monitor, picked out Keith's flight information, and groaned. Delayed thirty minutes. Why hadn't she thought to call and verify arrival times before she left?

Her eyes scanned the rows of plastic chairs. Finally she spied an empty spot tucked between an elderly gentleman and a tired-looking woman with two small children. Gillian worked her way through the crowd and slipped into the vacant seat.

She looked down at her oversized shoulder bag in disgust. There was no need to look inside; she knew the contents by heart: one battered make-up purse, a circular brush, a few loose pieces of cinnamon gum, one broken umbrella, a pair of sunglasses, her wallet and checkbook, one Gumby key chain, and a few odd receipts...but not a single thing to read. Gillian had left the office in such a rush, it hadn't occurred to her to bring along a stack of files. Who knew the flight would be late? She settled back and wriggled in her hard plastic seat, trying unsuccessfully to get comfortable. There was nothing to do but wait.

Gillian glanced at the man beside her, who gave her a curt nod, then turned abruptly away. She shifted awkwardly and looked in the other direction as the young mother who had been sitting beside her tried desperately to rein in her two wild children. Across the aisle from them, the toddler had approached a man holding a baby and was yelling, "Hi-hi-hi-hi-hi!" while waving one chubby little fist. As the child's mother bent to retrieve him, the older child began to run in circles around the room, ducking in and out of the waiting crowd and crying, "Vrooooooooooom," with his arms stretched out at his sides in a reasonable imitation of an airplane.

Gillian watched with a great deal of amusement and not a little trepidation. Would her own life ever include children? There was a time when she wouldn't have doubted it. Her childhood dreams had included a loving husband, a station wagon, an enormous black lab named Maggie, and a house full of kids.

But somewhere along the line, she had stopped believing in the dream. She still *hoped* she would find someone, settle down, and get married...someday. Unfortunately, things never quite worked out in her relationships. Though when she started dating Keith, everyone told her that he was a prize. "Don't give up so easily this time, Gillian," Bridget had urged her. "You're not getting any younger, you know."

Gillian had laughed. "You're crazy. I have all the time in the world to meet someone."

"That's right," Bridget said seriously. "But only if you *try.*" Friends like Pam and Bridget sometimes questioned her reasons for breaking up with the guys she occasionally dated. Sometimes they even suggested that she might be avoiding commitment. "You're terrible, Gil. You never even give a guy a chance. Don't be so hard on this one. Keith is a really good guy."

So, "giving it a try" was exactly what she was doing. She didn't feel overwhelmingly attached to him, but they had been dating for only six months. As she watched the woman with her children, Gillian wondered what it would be like to have kids with Keith. She'd never seriously thought about it before. She wasn't even sure she wanted to have children anymore. There was her career to think of. Astronomy was an extremely competitive field. She certainly didn't want to be distracted. On the other hand...

She smiled tenderly as the woman scooped up her little "airplane" and planted a kiss on his tiny forehead.

"Vroom! Vroom!" the boy cried happily.

"Vroom to you, too!" his mother said with a patient laugh.

On impulse, Gillian reached into her purse and pulled out her wallet. Flipping through it, she pocketed several ATM receipts, ticket stubs, and empty gum wrappers before finally finding what she was looking for: a photograph of herself standing next to a tall, athletic-looking blond. The corners of her mouth turned up slightly as she studied the image of Keith's smiling face.

Looks could be deceiving, that was for sure. At first glance, her boyfriend appeared more like a typical beach bum than the high-powered lawyer the entire legal community knew him to be. Yet, with his winning smile and competitive spirit, he would be just as at ease spiking a volleyball as he was arguing a case. Keith could fit in, in any crowd. People liked him, and he liked people…including Gillian.

That he'd chosen her still surprised her. Keith Waterford could have any woman he wanted. She'd met him at one of the political fund-raisers her mother had made her attend during a visit to D.C. All the women at the gathering had been gossiping about the attractive lawyer who, Gillian was told—as if this were a critical bit of information—was a distant relative of a prominent political family from Massachusetts. At first, Gillian hadn't been interested, even though Keith had paid a considerable bit of attention to her at the fund-raiser. He was thirty-three, quite a bit older than her own twenty-six years. He was the same age as Max, and she was painfully aware of how that had turned out.

When Keith called her the week after the party, however, she decided to reconsider. At twenty-six years old, she still hadn't had a successful long-term relationship. During her high school years, she would eventually find fault with each of the boys who wanted to date her. None of them measured up to the impossible standard she had raised. They weren't smart enough, mature enough, kind enough. In short, they weren't *Max*.

Her parents' breakup hadn't made things any easier, either, although it hadn't really come as a shock. The two were so different, it still amazed her that they had ever fallen in love. Once, as she and her mother were unpacking at their second house in Arlington, Virginia, a teenaged Gillian mustered the courage to ask about her parents' courtship.

Her mother was sorting through a box of comfortable old linens and window treatments from the home their family no longer shared when Gillian asked the question. "Mom...what made you fall in love with Dad in the first place?" Her mom, obviously flustered, quickly repacked the box of curtains that would not fit any of the windows in the new house.

"Oh, Gillian," her mom brushed the question aside and kept burrowing in the carton beneath her hands. "That was a long time ago. It's water under the bridge."

"Mom, please." Gillian stood up straight and stared at her. For once, she didn't want to the let the subject go. "I really want to know," she continued earnestly. Emma stopped unpacking, slowly laid down the stack of towels in her arms, and lowered herself onto a stool at the breakfast bar.

"Your father is a brilliant man, Gillian," she said slowly. "You know that, don't you?"

Gillian nodded solemnly, never taking her eyes from her mother's face.

"When I first met him...I thought he was everything I wanted in a man: intelligent—no, more than that, he was a *genius*. Powerful, mysterious. Very attractive, too. Best of all, he saw me as a person, not just as a potential wife. He respected my work; he respected *me*. I thought that there wasn't anything we couldn't handle together."

"I don't understand." Gillian dug at the shag carpet with one toe. "What happened, then?"

"Oh, Gilly!" Her mother reached out and took her by the hands, pulling her daughter into her lap. After being dragged away from the home she loved at seventeen-and-a-half, Gillian wasn't much in the mood to be held anymore. But for a moment, she allowed herself the comfort of her mother's arms. "A lot of things happened," Emma carefully explained. "There's a lot more to marriage than what you see on the surface. Your father and I...well, we didn't agree about a lot of other things. *Important* things."

Gillian nodded. "Like his working so much, huh? And religion?"

Her mom looked surprised. "Well, that's part of it, yes. You knew that?"

"I knew a lot of things. I heard you and Dad arguing."

"Oh, baby..." Emma's face fell, and she held her daughter close. "We didn't mean for you to hear that. We tried to keep our problems to ourselves."

"Well, you didn't do a very good job," Gillian said in a low voice. She didn't intend for her words to sound so mean, but she couldn't help it.

Her mom looked shocked at Gillian's tone, but she simply nodded. "I'm sorry, Gilly. Your father and I are both sorry...."

"Then, why didn't you make it work? Why didn't you and Dad just tell *each other* you were sorry?"

Emma shook her head. "It's complicated, Gilly."

"But—"

"Now, honey, listen. Do you want to know what happened, or not?"

Gillian clamped her mouth shut and nodded.

Emma took Gilly's hand and squeezed her fingers. "Life isn't easy, Gilly. You need to know that. Things don't always turn out the way you think they will." She thought for a moment. "Everything was fine between your father and me before we got married. But then a lot of things changed. For one thing, after a couple of years, I decided to go back to church. I hadn't thought much about my faith since I was a kid, but it was important to me to rediscover what I believed. I wasn't sure what it meant to follow God, but I committed myself to finding out. Your father...well, your father lumps spiritual beliefs in with the supernatural. He won't believe in anything that can't be scientifically proven. It put us on very different spiritual planes, which in turn put a lot of stress on our relationship. It wasn't our only problem. But not sharing this one thing made it even harder to find common ground in other areas." She paused to take a breath.

"After we'd been married for little more than a year, I realized that your father and I had very different expectations for our marriage. One of the reasons he liked my work so much was that he knew it would keep me busy...and out of his way while he did his own studies. He really is a genius, Gilly. I haven't always agreed with his conclusions about the nature of the universe, but he's done some incredible research." She paused, deep in thought, then said in a low voice, "His research has always come first."

"Before us." It wasn't a question.

Her mother sighed. "Yes. Before us. It wasn't always that way, but over the years things got increasingly worse. I knew it was hard on you, never seeing your dad. It was hard on me, too. I argued with him about it, but that just made things worse. Over the years, your father began to see me as a nag. Eventually, he stopped loving me."

"Oh." Gillian thought about this for a minute. "Did he stop loving me, too?"

Emma looked at her tenderly, and her eyes welled up with

tears. "Oh no, sweetheart! *No.* I promise you, your father loves you the best he knows how."

"Really?" Gilly played with the small emerald ring on her mother's hand, the one Emma had started wearing in place of her wedding band. "Mom, maybe he loves you the best he knows how, too."

"Well," Emma hugged her daughter tight, "maybe that's true. I don't know." The two sat together in silence for several minutes before she spoke again. "Gillian, I'm not saying that separating was the best thing for your father and me to do. The truth is, I don't *know* what's right for us anymore. All I know is, I love you. And I'm trying to do the best I can for us. Can you understand that?"

"Um. I guess."

"Oh, Gilly." Emma gave her one last squeeze. "Just be careful when you get older, okay?" she said wistfully. "Remember, it takes a lot to make a marriage work. It's not all about chemistry and good feelings. I'm not saying you shouldn't marry someone you feel good about. You *have* to feel strongly toward him to love him. But you also have to be sure he's someone you can be with, even through the tough times. You have to be certain that you agree about the most important things in life: like God, and family, and how you are going to love each other...and your children. Can you remember that, Gillian—?"

"Gillian? *Gillian?*"

"What?" Gillian blinked against the bright lights of the airport terminal. Who was shaking her arm? "Mom?" Slowly, the features of the figure beside her began to slip into focus.

"Come on, Sleeping Beauty," a deep voice said with a laugh. "Mom'll take you home."

"Keith?" Gillian shook her head vigorously, trying to clear her confusion. "Oh, my gosh! I just had the weirdest dream."

"Hmm. I guess *so*," Keith said seriously. He took Gillian by the hands and pulled her to her feet. "I can't wait to hear it."

She brushed the wrinkles from her corduroy shirt and wool skirt. "Umm, I don't know, Keith," she said slowly. "I'm not sure I can remember it."

"Sure you can!" He shouldered his carry-on bag and smiled broadly. "Come on. I'll play Dr. Freud, and you can be my patient."

"I don't think so—"

"Aw, come on. It'll be fun, Gillian," he urged.

As they began to wind their way toward baggage claim, Gillian stared sullenly at the carpet beneath her feet. What could she possibly say to him? *"Well, Keith, I was dreaming about this conversation I had with my mom. But it wasn't really a dream. It happened about eight years ago. We were talking about marriage, and love, and what it takes to make things work. And she said—"* No, that would never do. She wasn't ready to talk about marriage and love. Not yet. Not with Keith. "I'm sorry. My mind's kind of foggy," she said stiffly. "How was your flight?"

"Sure, Gillian, changing the subject?..." Keith said, a little too cheerfully. "It's okay." He gave her a big smile and turned away. As they walked on together in silence, Gillian felt terrible. She wasn't telling the truth, and she was sure Keith knew it. But thankfully, he wasn't going to push the issue. She fell into step beside him and tucked her hand into the crook of his arm. "Hey, Keith?" She managed a lopsided smile.

"Yeah, Gil?"

"Umm...it's good to have you home."

Six

> The relation of faith between subject and object is unique in every
> case. Hundreds may believe, but each has to believe by himself.
>
> W. H. AUDEN, "GENIUS AND APOSTLE," THE DYER'S HAND, 1962

July 12, 1987

Before I started kindergarten—back when I was five or so, I guess—
my dad used to take me out at night to watch the stardust.

We didn't go very often, and we couldn't go just any old time.
Only on special nights, when the sky was clear and the moon was
tucked away behind the Earth's shadow. That's when it would
appear: a ribbon of milky white dust that stretched high across the
heavens.

Of course, now I know that what we were looking at was the
Milky Way. But at the time, it was a magical, unexplainable thing—
this beautiful band of flickering light. Together we would sit, side-by-
side, on nothing but a blanket of grass, far from the city's lights.
Sometimes he'd bring a pair of binoculars or even a telescope. But
that was later. In the beginning, we used nothing but our eyes.

Mostly we were quiet. But every once in a while, Daddy would
point out a sea goat or a centaur or a flying horse and whisper its
name in my ear. Those are the only times I can remember Daddy
acting like a kid. He seemed in awe then. He wasn't like that at
work, behind his telescope, where he tried so hard to be in control.
Everything then was about facts and data, radio waves and Hubble's

law. Only when we were out, away from the lab, could he seem to really see the stars.

When I got older, it was important to Dad that I know all the statistical facts about the stars: their magnitude and type, color and size. I don't know why. Maybe it was just that I was growing up, and he wanted me to be like him. It wasn't so bad at first. Learning all that stuff was interesting, too. But I liked it better when there was a story behind the stars, when there was something to dream about and not just to know. After a while I got tired of it, and Dad got tired of me. Things weren't the same between us after that.

Last night, I was lying awake, thinking about those stars and wondering if, after all these years, they still looked the same. It's been a long time since I bothered to even look—I mean really look, not as a scientist, but just as a person. The more I thought about it, the more it bothered me. So finally, I decided to go out and see it for myself.

Sneaking out wasn't hard to do. Dad sleeps like a bear in hibernation, and Mom's away at one of her political bashes. It's a good thing, too, or I never would have gotten out of the house. I didn't go too far, anyway. I couldn't take the car—I don't have my license yet, and I doubt that even Dad would sleep through that much noise. So I just ran out to the main road and headed down toward the Gillys' field, about half a mile away.

By the time I got to the meadow, the Gillys' lights were out. No one was up except Elvis the cat, who was prowling the field looking for mice. It wasn't as far from the township lights as the places Dad used to take me as a kid. But at least it was a wide, open space, and I felt really free, for the first time in a long time.

The first thing I noticed out there was how quiet the sky was. I know that's a strange thought, but there you have it. When I look at something really awesome, like the Atlantic Ocean or the Grand Canyon, I always listen to the roar of the waves or the echo of the wind and think about what it sounds like to be so big. But the stars don't make a noise. At least, not one I can hear from here, anyway. Last night, I wished that I could fly up to the stars and just listen. What would I hear up there? Fire crackling on the face of the stars? The sound of wind? Is there wind in space?

Pretty soon, the Gillys' cat came and crawled into my lap, and then it wasn't so quiet anymore. But it was peaceful still, sitting there, looking up at the stars with Elvis on my knees, snoring like an old man.

After a while, I started getting cold. But for some reason, I just couldn't make myself get up. The more I looked into the sky, the more things I noticed—constellations I knew like I knew my own name, and beyond them, an ocean of stars I'd never noticed before. I wondered what made the stars keep moving. Why do the planets follow their orbits? Where did they come from? Where did I come from? And was it the same place? I kept my fingers buried in Elvis's thick fur and tried to imagine what it all meant. Dad seems to have his theories. Mom, too. And Max. Everyone but me.

That thought made me pretty nervous, like I was supposed to know. All of a sudden, the sky seemed a lot bigger...and scarier. Mom says a lot of people claim that they're afraid God might not exist, but she believes most of us are really afraid that he does. I think maybe she's right, because the more I thought about God, the more terrifying he seemed. Mom says that, yeah, he's terrifying, but there's more to it than that. She says that God cares about me, that he sent his son to earth because he loves me. Part of me wants to believe it, but I'm not even sure what it all means.

Dad says there isn't a God. I used to think he said it just to make Mom mad, but I'm pretty sure it's what he really believes. He likes things that can be explained, and he avoids anything that can't. Like me. Daddy couldn't figure me out. I loved the stars, once. I was good at memorizing all the stuff he told me about them. But one day, I just stopped trying. It wasn't fun for me anymore, and no matter what I said, I couldn't make him understand why. Feelings are funny things, *though. They're hard to explain. People aren't so easy to figure out, either. Neither is God, I guess.*

I don't know if I have to have all the answers, like my Dad does. Mom says that it's enough for her to know some of them…that it's enough to know that a thing can be true, even if it doesn't have to be…and to choose to believe.

I just don't know yet if it's enough for me.

June 27, 1997

"Hey, Max. I finished working through these calculations, and I was wondering if you wanted me to—" Gillian broke off at the sight of his shadowed face. Under the cold fluorescent lighting, his skin looked pale and sallow. Large, dark rings encircled his usually bright blue eyes. From behind his desk, he stared, expressionless, through the open window. "Max, what's the matter?" she asked quietly.

"Huh?" He tore his eyes away from the view of the campus and looked at her as if she had spoken Greek. "Oh, Gilly. It's you." His rigid expression softened at the sight of her. "What's that you said?"

"I asked what was bothering you." Gillian tucked her file folder beneath one arm and seated herself across from him. "You look like you haven't slept."

"Oh, I'm fine." He tried to sound confident, but his tone was less than reassuring. Gillian stared at his denim shirt, which looked like it had just been pulled from a tiny corner of his suitcase and could use a good ironing. Not that she was dressed any better. Her white, square-neck tee and celery-green capri pants were flattering, but hardly professional attire. Still, at least she was well groomed. She gave Max a scrutinizing look.

"You don't sound very convincing. Are you sleeping okay, really?"

"Gilly—" Max shook his head.

"I know, I know—you're fine. Sorry." She laid her folder down and raised her suntanned arms in surrender. "None of my business." He didn't have to tell her twice. Gillian didn't appreciate people prying into her affairs. No doubt, Max didn't like it either. With a businesslike nod, she turned back to the matter at hand. "I guess that means you're ready to go over these calcul—"

"Are you happy, Gilly?" Max broke in. She looked up to find him staring again, this time at her. It was more than a little unnerving. Uneasily, she crossed one leg over the other, trying to find a more comfortable position.

"We-ell. Most of the time. As happy as anyone, I suppose," she said slowly. She didn't like the way this conversation was turning. "Why do you ask?"

Max leaned his elbows on the desk and peered at her intently. "No, I mean *really* happy."

Gillian shrugged and tried to look away, but his eyes drew hers like a magnet. He was making her feel like a bug under a microscope. "I guess," she said noncommittally. "I have pretty much everything I want or need, if that's what you mean."

"Well," he said as if considering her answer. "I'm not sure it is."

Gillian tried to read Max's features, but his face was an impenetrable mask. Where was he going with this line of questioning? And what had she done to open herself up to this kind of interrogation, anyway? "What's this about, Max?" A snatch of conversation drifted through her mind. What was it Bridget had said? *"He just asked what the guy was like, was he good to you, did you love him...."*

"Max, is this about Keith?" she ventured uneasily. "Are you asking about my relationship with him?"

At that, Max sat up straight. Gillian couldn't help noticing that he appeared more than a little interested at this turn in the conversation. "Actually, I wasn't thinking *specifically* of him. But now that you mention it, how *are* things between you and Keith?"

Disturbed by the intimate question, Gillian rolled her chair back and tried to appear interested in a bookcase filled with technical papers. "Oh, Max. I really don't think this is an appropriate discussion for us to ha—"

"I'm not asking you as your supervisor, Gilly," he said gently but firmly. His eyes sought hers, demanding a response. "I'm asking you as a friend."

"As a friend?" Gillian shifted nervously. She couldn't help but wonder at his motivation. Hadn't they always been friends? Yes, certainly that is what they had been. Nothing more. She had no reason to think he was expressing anything other than a casual interest. "Well, I guess I'd have to say that we're—" She hesitated. How *were* things going between her and her boyfriend? "Yes, Keith and I are doing well. We're compatible. We care about each other. We're headed in the same direction." The sound of her own words made her angry. Why was it so hard to justify her relationship all of a sudden? Why did her response sound so flat? How dare Max ask such a thing in the first place! A trace of irritation crept into her voice. "Does that answer your question?"

At first, Max did not respond. And Gillian's emotions swung from anger to distress. She stared at him nervously. "Max? Come on. What's this all about?"

Max rubbed one rough hand across his stubbled jawline and let out a deep sigh. "I don't really know how to say this, Gilly. The truth is, you were right. I haven't been sleeping well at all."

Suddenly, any shred of composure she might have retained was in danger of slipping away. Her heart welled up with unwelcome concern. Was Max ill? In trouble? "What's the matter?" she asked anxiously. It was amazing how quickly she had come to care about this man again. It was as if he had never gone away.

He gazed at her with fathomless blue eyes that seemed to pull her into their depths. "Well...because I'm—"

Gillian caught her breath. If something terrible were to happen to Max, she didn't know what she'd do.

"—because I'm worried about you."

With a great whoosh, Gillian expelled the lungful of air she'd been holding in. "Me?" She tried to imagine what on earth he could be referring to. "That's ridiculous! Why would you need to worry about me?"

"I'm not totally sure," he said solemnly. "That's what I'm trying to figure out." His eyes furrowed together in an expression of concern, giving him the air of an overprotective older brother. When she was younger, if he had done that, it would have been endearing to Gillian, but the image did not please her any longer.

Gillian met his eyes over the desk. "Max, please. Speak English. I really don't know what you're talking about."

"I don't know...." He shook his head, as if unable to find the words to express himself. "I started worrying the first day I saw you. Don't get me wrong. It was *great* to see you, Gilly. But you seem...different, somehow."

By the tone of his voice, Max didn't consider it to be a change for the better. His statement sounded almost like a criticism and Gillian felt deflated. As a teenager, she had dreamed of seeing Max again, of showing him how much she'd grown up, how she'd changed. Now that dream had come true—she *had* grown up and found him again. So what would cause him to act so concerned?

"Different...how?" she asked. Her voice was little more than a whisper. It didn't seem possible that after all these years, his opinion would matter so much. But it did.

Max looked confused. "I wish I knew. It's hard to explain," he said uneasily. "I know it's been ten years since we've seen each other. I realize that you've grown up. But you just seem…"

"Seem what, Max?"

He spoke slowly, as if the words pained him. "Shut down, I guess. Closed. The Gilly I knew was open and trusting. At least toward me."

Tears threatened to spring from Gillian's eyes, but she fought them back. "The Gilly you knew was a naive child!" She tried to sound tough, but his accusation had wounded her deeply.

His eyes were full of compassion as he gazed deeply into hers. "I'm sorry. It's just that you used to be so happy—"

"Max. I was just a *girl*. Now I'm an adult."

"I think it's more than that." He reached across the desk to touch her fingers, ever so gently. "What happened to you, Gilly?"

Gillian snatched her hand back, as if a snake had bit her. "*Life* happened, Max," she snapped. It wasn't any of his business. Max, her dad…more people than she could count, had let her down. Even worse, she'd let other people down, too. Getting close to someone didn't seem worth the risk anymore, but she wasn't about to discuss this with Max. "I wish you wouldn't make me sound like such a basket case," she said, managing to match the cool, controlled tone she had spoken with earlier. "There's nothing wrong with me, really. I'm just not the same Gillian you remember. What's wrong with that?"

"Nothing," Max admitted. "If you're happy."

Gillian frowned. "Again with the 'happy'? Max, believe me. I'm *happy*, okay?"

"Pardon me for saying so, but you don't *look* happy."

Her scowl deepened. "I will *not* pardon you for saying so.

And I *am* happy. So there." Gillian knew her words sounded childish, but she could not stop them. They seemed to fly off her tongue of their own accord. She groaned inwardly. No wonder he didn't think she had changed for the better. She was even more immature than the child he once knew.

"If you say so," Max said diplomatically. "I won't argue. But I can't help worrying about how you're dealing with life."

Those were fighting words if she'd ever heard any. Not that Gillian needed any further invitation to fight. The gloves were already on and laced up tight. "Now what is *that* supposed to mean?" she ground out testily.

"Just that...well, life is hard, Gilly," he said simply. He rested his hands casually on the desk, his fingers interlocked. He looked more like a salesman trying to sell annuities than a former heartthrob throwing her life into emotional turmoil.

"You think I don't know that?" Her parents had split up when she was a teenager; she'd been dragged from city to city by her politically active mother; at twenty-six years old she'd never had a single long-term relationship...and he was trying to tell *her* that life wasn't easy?

"I'm sure you do know it," Max said calmly. "It's just that, I'm afraid you don't have the resources that can help you deal with it."

Gillian blinked. Now he just wasn't making any sense at all. "Resources."

Max grinned sheepishly. "Yeah, resources. There I go, talking like a scientist. I suppose that's because you're a scientist, too. I feel like maybe I can get away with it. But this isn't about facts and figures, Gilly," he said more seriously. "I'm talking about the heart."

Resources. The heart. What on earth was Max getting at? Gillian stared at him blankly.

"I'm not making any sense here, am I?" he said regretfully. "I guess what I'm trying to say is that I care about you. That's why I'm worried. You mentioned last week that you weren't sure you agreed with me about God being the Creator of the universe. Maybe I'm assuming too much here—and please, forgive me if I am—but I'm guessing that means you don't have a relationship with him."

Max's eyes betrayed his sadness, and Gillian squirmed a bit under his gaze.

"I know in my own life, I'd be lost if I didn't have God to turn to when things get tough." He spoke clearly and honestly. "I can't tell you how much it means to me," he said earnestly, "to know that God loves me. That he's with me whenever I struggle to know what to do, what to say." He laughed wryly. "Like now."

Gillian's mind was spinning. A relationship with God? Was he kidding? It had been a long time since anyone other than her mother had suggested she might need such a thing. The prospect was both daunting and confusing. If God was God, then he had the entire universe at his command. What would he want with her? The idea was preposterous.

"Max, even if God exists, I don't think he wants to be bothered with my petty little problems," she said forcefully, but she could not deny the wistful feeling that came with wondering if what he suggested might actually be true.

"Oh, sw—" Max stopped himself. Gillian glanced at him sharply. What was he just going to say? Had he almost called her sweetheart? Impossible. Or was it? But before she could question him, Max had already composed himself and moved on. "I know it's hard to believe. It was hard for me to grasp, too. I still struggle with it from time to time. But honestly, Gilly, he does care. It says so all over the Bible. It's not that he cares about those petty little things, I guess, so much as it is that he cares about us. You and me."

"You, maybe," Gillian allowed reluctantly. How could anyone not care about Max?

"No," Max insisted firmly. "You, too. Here, let me read you something." He reached into an upper desk drawer and pulled out a small, worn leather-covered book which Gillian took to be a Bible. "Here we go. Matthew 28:20: 'Surely I am with you always, to the very end of the age.' And it's not because we deserve it, either. Listen. Romans 5:8: 'But God demonstrates his own love for us in this: While we were still sinners, Christ died for us.' You see, Gilly? It's right here, in black and white."

Gillian stared at her hands as she felt something stirring in her heart. She wanted to believe him, she really did. But, could she face the risk of opening herself up once again? What if it wasn't true? What if God didn't exist? What if he didn't accept her, after all? What if her doubts, her questions, were too much to forgive? Could she survive being left all alone once again?

"God is there for you, Gilly. All you have to do is let him in," Max assured her gently. "Wouldn't it be nice to have someone you could depend on? Someone who would love you and take care of you and be there for you? Always? Just like Jesus said?"

Despite the ninety-degree weather, Gillian felt a sudden chill. Somehow, Max had, with just a few simple sentences, neatly summarized the deepest longings of her heart. How had he known? Nervously, she licked her parched lips.

"That's a nice fairy tale, Max," she said coolly, trying to sound disinterested. But despite herself, Gillian felt a tug at her heart strings. She thought the words would anger him, but Max appeared undisturbed.

"I think it's more than a fairy tale," he said matter-of-factly. Gillian stood and pushed her chair back roughly, causing it to roll across the smooth office floor and plow into a shelf of books. Max watched with interest as she began to pace. Gillian scrambled for the words to justify her position. "Come on,

Max. Be serious. Just what do you expect me to believe?"

"Maybe the evidence?"

"Max, you know there's no solid evidence. You said so yourself."

"I said there was no *definitive* evidence. There's a difference," he argued.

"I've already told you, I don't know what I believe."

"I know. But you could find out." How could he seem so calm when she felt so disturbed?

"Why would I want to, Max? Give me one good reason," she said testily.

Max stood and came to her side. "Peace. Hope. Joy," he said gently, reaching out to take her hand.

Gillian watched his fingers close around hers and felt her fury begin to fade. This time she did not pull away. She should be furious. But Max's words were spoken with such compassion, her anger melted away.

"That's *three* things," Gillian said grumpily, but the words did not sound forceful as she'd intended; they sounded comical.

A hint of a smile tugged at the corners of Max's mouth. "You don't say? And I'm just getting started."

"Okay, Max," she sighed. "I'll admit it. I don't feel a lot of peace right now, and I don't even remember the last time I did. But the truth is, I've never really thought of God as being the answer to that. Dad never believed in an omnipotent force, and he instilled in me a pretty healthy skepticism."

Max nodded. "I can understand."

"So, you see, it isn't easy for me."

"I know, Gilly." He reached out and brushed a finger across her furrowed brow, his touch as light as a butterfly's wing. "I didn't mean to push. It's just that…I really care about you. I want you to be happy. You know that, don't you?"

Tears welled up in Gillian's eyes once more as she thought of the days when she had longed to hear those words from him. But even if he had said them at the time, they couldn't have been an expression of anything more than friendship. Exactly as they were now.

"I know, Max. I do." She smiled weakly. "And...I'll think about it. Honestly, I'm really not sure I believe what you say is true, but I think I'd like it if I found out that it was."

Max smiled, the corners of his eyes crinkling along their familiar lines, and he squeezed Gillian's hand, which she suddenly realized he still held. He looked at her tenderly, and as they lingered, her head began to spin. All at once Gillian panicked. She withdrew her hand with a jerk and began to back away.

"Look, Max...I've got to go. There's a whole stack of papers on my desk, and if I'm going to be any use to you at all, I think I should—"

He watched her pull back, a look of confusion deposing his previous expression of tenderness. "Gilly, *now* what's going on?" Max said in exasperation.

"Nothing!" Gillian lied, trying to regain her composure. She reached for her folder and began to make a hasty retreat. "I just—"

But Max wasn't going to let it go. "Ever since the day I got here, you've been acting like a skittish horse, rearing up and running away when I get near. Come on, don't deny it. You know what I'm talking about." He followed her to the door. "What's this all about?"

"Max, I just don't think it's appropriate for you and me to get too close," she said, a sound of desperation creeping into her voice. Her breathing grew labored. Max was standing terribly near now. If she wanted to, she could reach out and touch the rough fabric of his shirt where the buttons met. Every instinct, every muscle in her body cried out for her to step away, but she didn't want to appear any more "skittish."

A muscle in his jaw twitched. "Because of Keith?" he said.

Gillian stared at him. His face looked so strong and masculine. A muscle twitched in his jaw. "Yes." She gladly seized the excuse. "Because of Keith. Okay?" She turned as if to head for the door, but Max moved, too, partially blocking her path. Gillian forced herself to remain where she was standing.

"And what else?"

"Max! For crying out loud!" A sigh of frustration escaped her lips. She could hear the strain in her own voice. "Why does there have to be something else?" Why did he have to keep pushing the issue? Couldn't he just leave her alone?

"Because," he insisted, "I have a lot of female friends who are married or romantically involved, and not one of them has to run away every time I come into the room!"

"That's not what I'm doing!" Drawing upon anger to save her from crying, Gillian planted two fists on her hips and squared off against him.

"It's not?" Max demanded.

"You *know* it's not!" she said hotly.

"Do I?"

"Auuuugh!" Gillian let out a small cry of frustration. Obviously sensing that he had pushed too far, Max leaned back a fraction of an inch, giving her room to breathe. "Look, can we just drop this, please? You're making me really uncomfortable, and I have to get back to work—" Gillian turned her back on him, grabbing her chance at escape.

"Gilly, come on—"

She shook her head and continued out the door.

"Gilly, wait! I'm not through talking!"

"Well, I am. Okay, Max?" She'd had enough. There was a time when she would have allowed herself to be at Max's beck and call, but those days were long gone. He was being kind to her. But that wasn't enough. She was tired of being his little buddy, his little pal. Her world didn't revolve around him, around what *he* wanted. She had her own life now. One that *didn't* include Max Bishop. He wasn't in her life to stay. He never had been. "If you want to talk to someone, why don't you go call Bridget?" she said sharply.

"What? *Bridget?*" He looked at her as though she was out of her mind. "But what does Bridget have to do wi—?"

Good grief! Where had those words come from? That wasn't what she felt, was it? "Nothing!" Gillian said quickly. "She doesn't have anything to do with this! I just…I mean—" She felt a sinking feeling in the pit of her stomach, but there was nothing she could do to take the words back. "Look, let's just forget it, okay? I'll talk to you later," she said firmly and closed the door behind her.

Out in the hallway, she clung to the metal doorknob, her heart welling up with regret.

At least I hope I'll talk to you later, she thought sadly. *The question is, are you gonna want to talk to me?*

Seven

Friends provoked become the bitterest of enemies.
BALTASAR GRACIAN, THE ART OF WORLDLY WISDOM, 1647

July 18, 1987

I can't believe this is happening. I wish I'd never heard of that creepy old Matt Ross or his cousin, Chris. I wish he'd go right back to Chicago. I wish he'd never come here at all. Maybe then I wouldn't have gotten into this mess in the first place.

So here's the deal: Jenny DeWhitt, my best friend, hates me. And I can't say that I blame her, although I never meant to do anything to hurt her—I swear it. In fact, the whole stupid thing was her idea. You'd think she'd cut me a little slack for that, but no such luck.

Ever since she sat next to Matt in English last semester, Jenny's had it bad. She calls me up all the time and tells me every little thing about him. As a result, I am a veritable fountain of Matt Ross trivia. Go ahead and test me. I know that he wears a size ten and a half shoe and that his ideal woman is Daisy Duke from Hazzard County. I know that his GPA is 2.85 and that his middle name is Alfonso. I even know that he pulled a groin muscle last year at the lake while he was water-skiing. Like this is information I even want to know?

Sometimes she even writes her name with his: Jenny Ross. It gets pretty sickening after a while, and I want to tell her that it makes her sound like she should be sewing an American flag or something. But

I never do. I know how it feels to care about somebody, to wish more than anything that he would like you back. Jenny and I are in different boats, though. My love is one of those tragic, Shakespearean kinds that can never be fulfilled. (Except, of course, I don't plan to poison myself. But...you get the picture.) Jenny, on the other hand, has been working on her Matt Plan for almost a year. The Matt Plan has three phases:

Phase I: Setting the Bait. Otherwise known as, Getting-Matt-to-Notice-I'm-Alive. This was a thoughtfully planned and carefully executed maneuver that involved countless hours of wardrobe, makeup, and hair consultation with her sister Marta and (you guessed it) yours truly.

Phase II: The Hunt. Once the subject's attention was captured, it was time for the really fun part (fun for Jenny, anyway). At this point in The Plan, basic flirtation began. This phase opened the door to endless telephone discussions that sprang from the ever-critical questions: "What-Do-You-Think-He-Meant-By...?" and "Did-You-See-the-Way-He...?" I was also called upon at this point to distract Matt's cousin Chris. Those two have been inseparable ever since he moved here, which hasn't made Jenny's and my work any easier, let me tell you. I accomplished the goal by sitting next to Chris at lunch and asking him questions about the football team (thereby freeing up Matt to flirt with Jenny). After the first question, all I ever had to do was mumble "Mm-hmm" every six or seven seconds. The guy is like a big talking doll...just wind him up and watch him go.

Phase III: Going for the Kill. In this the final, and most controversial, phase of The Matt Plan, Jenny had determined that we should divide and conquer. This was a problem for me. It wasn't the dividing part that I argued with. Matt's a nice enough guy, at least I thought so. Nicer than his cousin, anyway. I figured he was better off getting divided from Chris every once in a while. But I certainly didn't want to conquer Chris, myself! Jenny thinks we'd be cute together, and I'm flattered in a way. He is adorable. He's kind of funny, too. I sort of liked him at first. But really, he's not my type. He's not all that smart. And his interests are pretty limited. Once you get to know him, the guy is dull as a fence post, unless of course football is your religion.

The good news is, I never really had to deal with Phase III. The bad news is, that's because The World As I Know It came to an end during Phase II.

If it hadn't been for Jenny's birthday, we might have made it through the summer just fine. But she decided to have this big ol' Birthday-fest in her parents' backyard. I'm surprised her parents agreed, but they must have felt guilty about spending all that money on their oldest daughter, 'cause they caved. Doesn't really matter, I guess, if they can afford it.

So, there we were: Jenny, Matt, Chris, and I, and about twenty or so of our closest friends. There was pizza and swimming and dancing (although nobody shook even one little booty until Jenny convinced her parents to go inside—where, of course, they watched from the living room window). I was doing my best to keep Chris busy, saying things like, "So, tell me again why you think the coach is going to play you more?" and, "How do you think the team is going to do this year?" when some wise guy held a plastic Coke bottle up over his head and started calling out a play. Naturally, Chris started yelling and ran out for the pass.

I was waiting and watching and trying to figure out this whole testosterone thing, when Matt came up and stood next to me. I didn't think much about it. We always hang out together around Jenny. I know so much about him, it would have been pretty hard not to become friends. We talked for a few minutes, and then he said he wanted to go check out the pool.

There was nothing else going on, so I followed him. But as soon as we crossed the little dance floor Jenny's dad had made, Matt slipped his arms around my waist and started moving his feet back and forth to the music. It kind of freaked me out, and I started to

101

look all around us. "Hey, if you want to dance, I bet you Jen—"

"No, not Jenny. I want to dance with you," he said. And he said it like he really meant it.

I just stared at him.... I couldn't have been more surprised. At first, I started to pull away. But then I saw the look on his face, and for the first time, I realized that a boy liked me—I mean, really liked me. And just for a second, I wondered what it would be like to let him like me. I didn't really think about what it would be like to care about him—not yet—even though Matt is pretty darn likable himself. I just was all caught up in thinking about how it would feel to be loved, just as I am...just once. And so I relaxed, just for a second, and leaned my head against his shoulder, which felt really strong and warm, and smelled good besides....

And then he spun me around, and I saw Jenny's face. It was greenish white and cold looking, and I wondered in that first split second if maybe she had eaten something that had made her sick. And then I realized that the thing making her sick was me.

I tried to talk to her after that, but she just ran into her room and locked it. Everyone at the party knew that something had happened, but they didn't know what. Her parents begged me to tell them what was wrong, but I didn't have the guts. I tried to get Jenny to let me into her room, but she wouldn't even talk to me through the door. Matt and Chris left soon after that. Chris has a license, so they didn't even have to wait for a ride. Pretty soon, everyone else started going, too. I didn't call my folks, though. I walked home instead. It's a two-and-a-half mile walk, and even though it was a summer night, it got to be pretty cold. But after the kind of friend I'd been, I figured cold was just what I deserved.

Some people say that love makes the world go 'round. I doubt I'll ever find out for myself. Relationships are just too hard. I don't think I'll ever get there.

And if this is what they do to people, I'm not sure I even want to.

With slim, pale fingers, Gillian pinched the bridge of her nose and squinted her hazel eyes shut tight. Releasing her grip, she shook her head vigorously, sending her golden, shoulder-length hair flying. A moment later she opened her eyes and turned once more to the book she held in one hand. It was no use. The letters still danced across the page like ants marching to a picnic. She'd left her glasses at the office again. There would be little point in trying to read tonight.

It was a shame, too, because if there was ever a time when she needed a distraction, this was it. The day had been a complete disaster. After her fight with Max, she hadn't had a single moment of clear concentration. Originally, she planned to spend the afternoon analyzing data from other physicists who had been working on theories similar to Max's. But though she read through an entire stack of papers, the words and concepts had crossed and commingled in her mind until they formed one indistinguishable mess, just like the letters on the page now open before her. Gillian groaned. With nothing but her own miserable thoughts for company, she'd never be able to get to sleep.

"If you want to talk to someone, why don't you go call Bridget?" Where had *that* come from? What on earth had she been *thinking?* She sounded like…well, like a jealous shrew. But how could she be jealous? She had Keith. After failing at every other relationship she'd had over the past ten years, she had promised herself—not to mention Bridget, Pam, *and* her mother—that she was going to give this one a fair shot. Keith was sweet and kind and…safe. Infinitely safe. Something that Max definitely was *not.*

All right, so the thought of Max and Bridget dating was a bit disturbing. Admittedly, Gillian *had* been relieved to find out that Max had simply invited Bridget out for a cup of espresso and not dinner by candlelight. And though it would have been eternally wiser to keep her mouth shut, Gillian hadn't been able to resist the urge to warn Bridget away from the man who had stolen her own heart ten years before. But that didn't mean that she was—

All right, it did. She was jealous.

Gillian grabbed one of two overstuffed down pillows and punched it into a lumpy ball, which she placed behind her back. Settling back against the headboard, she wriggled her toes down into the deep, warm flannel sheets and squinted again at the book in her hand, a battered old copy of *Wuthering Heights,* which she now lifted close to her nose. Reading would surely help her forget her troubles.

On my re-entrance, I found Mr Heathcliff below. He and Joseph were conversing about some farming business; he gave clear, minute directions concerning the matter discussed, but

…but…but…but even if she was jealous, Gillian reasoned, wasn't that to be expected? Just because a person remembered her first crush fondly and harbored memories of dreams that had once lived, did that have to mean she still cared for the man? Certainly not. She forced her attention to the page, pushing back the worries that haunted her.

On my re-entrance, I found Mr. Heathcliff below.

No, no. She'd read that part already. She was still trying to find her place when she heard a solid rapping on her bedroom door.

"Oooooooooooh," she let out a low moan. *It might be just Pam. But it could also be Bridget.* "Come in," she said warily. As the door swung open, she fought the urge to sink back against her pillows and cover her head with her old patchwork quilt.

"Hi, Gillian," Bridget said stiffly. A light cotton robe was draped over her shoulders, barely covering her long T-shirt and boxer shorts. Her short, cropped curls were tousled, as though she had just crawled out of bed.

"Hey, Bridget," Gillian laid the book down and tried to greet her roommate as if there was no rift. "What's up? Couldn't sleep?"

"Nope." Bridget fell silent. Gillian had hoped that the tension between them would eventually subside, but by the look on Bridget's face that wasn't about to happen anytime soon. "I—uh—I ran into Max during lunch today."

"Oh." Gillian fumbled for words. The events of the day came tumbling back upon her like an avalanche. "You did." Her words and the voice with which she delivered them were equally dull.

"Yeah." Bridget's eyes flickered around the room, darting from the brightly colored rag rug to the antique-white walls to the stained pine vanity table…anything but Gillian's face. "And I was wondering if you could answer a question for me."

Gillian sat up straight, folded her legs Indian-style beneath the blankets and prepared for the worst. "Sure, Bridget," she said casually. "Shoot."

Bridget crammed her fists into the pockets of her robe and finally looked directly at her. "What did you say to Max about what happened between us?"

"Umm…" Gillian scrambled to find some way to explain. Initially, she had felt regret about the way she responded to Max simply because it was unfair and unkind to him. It was only later in the afternoon that she realized she had put her roommate in a difficult position as well. She'd been wondering how she might remedy the situation. But now, it looked like it was too late for damage control. She wished she'd said something to Max earlier in the day. But she certainly hadn't expected him to take the matter straight to Bridget!

"He knew that you and I had had some sort of fight," Bridget went on, not waiting for an answer.

Gillian tucked her comforter more tightly around her legs. "What did he say, exactly?"

"He just said that you seemed really uncomfortable when my name came up today. He wondered if something had happened between us."

"That's all he said?" Gillian couldn't believe her ears. Perhaps Max hadn't ratted on her after all.

"Yeah. What I'm wondering is, why did my name even come up in the first place?"

Again, Gillian tried to reason a way out of the question; there was no easy way to explain. But to her relief, Bridget once again pushed on without waiting for a response.

"More to the point, what *exactly* did you say to him about our fight?"

"Nothing, Bridget. Really."

"Are you sure?" Looking slightly relieved, the petite brunette sank into a slipcovered chair in the corner. "Because I'd feel ridiculous if I thought that Max knew I was interested in him." At this admission, Gillian's heart sank. But she knew better than to challenge Bridget's feelings this time. She decided to focus on the one issue she *could* handle.

"Are you kidding? What would I say to him? 'Oh, by the way, Bridget and I had a fight about you because we both like you'? No way. Not only is it *not* true, I'd look like an even bigger fool than you seem to think *you* would. Unh-unh. I didn't say a word."

"Well…" Bridget looked somewhat relieved, but a trace of tension still clouded her face. "Whatever. As long as you're sure you didn't say anything. But no matter what you claim, I still think you like him, Gillian."

For the briefest moment, Gillian actually considered pulling the blankets up over her head and burying her face beneath them. "Bridget, come on. Are we going to have this conversation again? I thought we worked through all of this."

The woman shook her head vigorously. "No. We didn't work through anything. How could we, Gillian?" Bridget's eyes accused her. "You're not being honest with me."

Gillian tried to shut out the bare emotion in her roommate's expression and to focus instead on her own sense of cool detachment. "Yes, I am, Bridget—"

"Gillian, please! Don't make me laugh." It didn't look like there was much chance of that. "It's so *obvious* that you're infatuated with him. I don't see why you can't just come out and say so. Don't you trust me?"

"But I *don't* like him!" The more she protested, the weaker it sounded.

"All right, all right." Bridget dragged one bare toe across the rug beneath her feet. "You've made your point. You're not admitting *anything*. I'm just saying I *know* you like the guy."

Gillian felt a renewed anger rising inside of her. Hadn't she already addressed the issue a dozen times? "Bridget, come on! I don't see why we have to fight over this."

"I'm not fighting," she protested. "*Max* was the one who seemed to think we were fighting—"

"Auuuugh!" Gillian made a face and clenched her jaw. "Bridget, don't *do* that. You do *too* know that we're fighting. We both know it. Why don't we just—"

Bridget looked at her innocently. "Yeah? Well we both know that you like Max, too. But you're not admitting *that*."

Gillian's patience was wearing thin. "That's enough, Bridget. You're putting words in my mouth."

"I'm just stating the truth," Bridget said coldly.

"Knock it *off*—" Gillian stopped herself and took a deep

breath. "Please." She managed to bring her frenzied emotions back under control. "Look, it's late, and this really isn't a good time for us to be getting into this. If you want to talk about it more tomorrow, we can. But right now, I'm just too tired."

"That's fine," Bridget said, stiffly pushing herself out of the old chair. "I need to get to bed, too. I just wanted to find out if there was anything I should know about your conversation with Max. I'll get out of your hair now." As she made her way toward the door, Gillian felt a wave of regret sweep over her.

"Bridget, please. Stop. I don't want to fight over a *guy!*"

"Don't you get it, Gillian?" Bridget turned and stared at her incredulously. "We're not fighting over a guy."

Max was so clearly the issue, it was hard for Gillian not to accuse her roommate of playing emotional games. "Then, what is this about?" she asked carefully.

"It's about you being a jerk." Bridget said simply. She spoke as smoothly and easily as if she had just commented that Gillian looked good in blue.

"Excuse me?"

Bridget ignored the contortions of Gillian's face and voice. "Gillian, I *know* you're not coming clean. Either you're lying to me about your feelings, or you're not being honest with yourself. Either way, you're not being a very good friend—to yourself, or to me. The thing is, you don't have to tell me anything you don't want to." Bridget fingered the soft material at the end of one sleeve. "I just wish you'd tell me if that was the case. I thought we were closer than this, that's all. Guess I was wrong." She shrugged and turned away. A second later, she was gone.

Late that night, long after Bridget had left her alone in her room, Gillian lay still and silent in her bed, considering what had been said. It had taken her weeks to admit that she felt jealous at all, even a simple jealousy that reflected only the past. But was she kidding herself? Were the feelings she had for Max actually, as Bridget proposed, far more than a memory?

Gillian flopped over onto her side and hugged one soft pillow close under her cheek. It wasn't that the possibility of carrying a torch for Max hadn't occurred to her. As distressing as the thought was, that at least was something she had considered before. No. Perhaps most disturbing of all was Bridget's brutally honest assessment of Gillian's relationships with her friends.

To those who knew her, it was no big secret that Gillian had problems with romantic relationships. She herself admitted she was more than a little gun-shy. The romances she enjoyed most were soothing, nonconfrontational, and somewhat superficial— such as the one she had with Keith. They were based on mutual respect and shared interests, not passion. It took a long time for problems to reveal themselves under such conditions. And, by maintaining a degree of detachment, Gillian always managed to extricate herself without any significant degree of suffering.

But, if Bridget's accusations were accurate, it would seem that her *modus operandi* for friendships was alarmingly similar. While she had remained vaguely aware of her own desire to avoid the "Max issue," Gillian had never intended to deliberately deceive Bridget about her feelings. Yet their relationship had clearly suffered, perhaps irreparably. She'd known for a long time that she liked to keep people at arm's length. But she'd never before thought of herself as being a bad friend.

Burrowing her face against the soft blue-and-white flannel pillowcase, Gillian tried to identify the source of her trouble. Was it her father's neglect? The loss of Max? Her failed friendship with Jenny? Mom and Dad's divorce? Had all these situations together instilled in her an inner fear that kept her from letting anyone get close? If so, was there any hope for her future?

Without warning, Max's words came back to haunt her. *"Life* is *hard, Gilly….I'm afraid it's harder on you than it needs to be.*" She had told him that she didn't appreciate being thought of as a basket case. But she was beginning to feel more and more like one.

But God? When she thought of a divine creator, Gillian's thoughts turned toward the heavens, not toward her own petty problems. If there really was a God, she couldn't imagine that he would be concerned about her little world. Although…Max seemed to think that he was. And so did Mom. Maybe it wouldn't hurt to find out more about it one of these days.

As she drifted off, Gillian wondered what it would be like to *know* God. Although she hadn't come to any real conclusions about him, somehow the mere thought seemed to bring her hope, and she was not alone with her miserable memories after all. Despite her earlier fears that she would never rest, she soon fell into a peaceful, dream-filled sleep.

Eight

*Intimacy requires courage because risk is inescapable.
We cannot know at the outset how the relationship will affect us.*
ROLLO MAY, *THE COURAGE TO CREATE*, 1975

July 20, 1987

I've been trying to reach her for days, but Jenny won't even come to the phone. I guess she told her mom what happened, because Mrs. D. acts pretty snippy toward me when I call. The next thing you know, she'll be telling my mom about the whole ugly scene. Then I'll be grounded for sure. I haven't gotten the official green light to go out with any guys yet. No doubt Mom would consider this little episode a subversion of her rules.

So much for dating. And...so much for being in love. Jenny's bubble was pretty much destroyed, thanks to me. And me...well, I haven't seen Max in days. Dad's been spending a lot of time at his office this week, getting ready for some conference, so Max has been meeting him there. Not that it would make any difference if he came here to our house. No matter how much I like him, it still isn't going to happen. It's just not. I wish I could forget about him altogether. I wish I could forget about all of them. Max, Dad...Jenny, too.

It's just so hard, not being what they want. Max apparently wants some beautiful co-ed. And, really, who can blame him? Dad wants a little version of himself. Mom wants me to become a

Christian, like her. And Jenny...well, Jenny just wanted me to be a good friend. Which I wasn't.

One thing's for sure. Relationships are a dangerous thing. You never know what's gonna happen. It's enough to make you think twice before getting close to anybody. I don't know what's worse—getting hurt or being the one that's done the hurting.

The other day while my mom was working at the kitchen table, she had the radio on and was listening to some program about a guy who went and lived in a cave for seven months. I don't know whether he was a monk or just a hermit....I wasn't really paying attention to what was going on. But I got to thinking about it later, and I've decided that maybe the guy had the right idea. There was no one to get in his way. He probably got to do whatever he wanted, whenever he wanted...although I suppose that doesn't mean so much when you're in a cave.

If I could do it right now, I'd go live in a cave, too. I wouldn't let anyone come see me, except Max, of course. Someone would send me supplies by mule every week. Just the basics: food and water, matches...and maybe Casey Kasem's Top 40 Countdown.

I could probably survive for a long time like that. Just me and Max and Casey Kasem, hangin' out in the cave and talkin' about life.

But for now, I'm stuck here in Princeton. Summer's half over already. Pretty soon I'll have to go back to Chat. Except this time, I won't have Jenny on my side. I'll have to face all the competition, the backstabbing all on my own. Oh, I have other friends, all right. But none as close as Jenny. By the time Jenny tells them what happened, they probably won't like me, either. Doesn't really matter, though. I guess I'm getting what I deserve.

I think I will miss Jenny, though. I wish she would forgive me. But it doesn't look like she's going to, and that's something I'm just going to have to live with. If I could go back in time and change it all, I would. But I can't. All I can do is try my best to keep it from happening again. No matter what it takes.

"That's it. No more interviews for me." Pam closed the door behind her with a resounding thud. "It's official," she said, dropping her briefcase on the floor. "I'm going to remain unemployed until the day I die."

"Alrighty," Gillian said, glancing over the top of her copy of *Sky and Telescope*. From where she lay, stretched out on the oversized camelback sofa, she could barely make out Pam's dark head. "It's nice to see that you're not being overly dramatic." She flopped her magazine down on top of the soft yellow cushions with their cheerful red rosettes.

"You think I'm kidding, Gil? It's dog-eat-dog out there." Pam stepped around the couch and into full view. Gillian studied her with a discerning eye. Dressed in a knee-length sand-colored jumper, stylish cotton stockings, and crisp white blouse, she looked professional and *in vogue*. If image played any factor at all, Gillian would have thought that her roommate would get the first job she applied for. "I'm exhausted." Pam flopped down into a threadbare, pinkish red armchair that looked as though it had seen far better days. "All I want to do tonight is sink into a hot bath and soak myself until I'm one big prune," she announced, kicking off her tailored, stacked-heeled Mary Janes.

"Ooo. Sounds lovely," Gillian said sarcastically, wishing she had thought of it first.

Pam arched her eyebrows at Gillian's tone. "The part about the bath, or me being a prune?"

"It's a tough call. Seriously, though...save me some hot water. I could use a good soak." She reached up with one hand and began to gently rub at the bound-up muscles in her neck. That's what she needed: a long, warm, soothing retreat from the world at large. She began a mental checklist: long vanilla candles, lilac bubble bath, the soft strains of Faure's *Pelleas et Melisande*....

"Pretty tense?" Pam sympathized, her deep blue eyes full of concern.

"Oh, my gosh." Gillian bit out a short laugh, but there was no humor in it. "You don't know the half of it."

"Still having a hard time with Bridget, huh?" Pam said knowingly.

"Yeah." Gillian nodded. She looked at her friend suspiciously. "Hey, maybe you *do* know the half of it. How did you hear about that? Has she talked to you?"

"As a matter-of-fact, she did, a little bit. Not that she would have had to, though, for me to notice. It's pretty obvious. You two have been moping around here like a couple of grounded teenagers."

"Yeah. Well. We've been fighting like teenagers, too," Gillian admitted guiltily. "I hate it."

"So make up, then." Pam reached forward and began to massage her aching feet.

"Wish I could," Gillian sighed. She did, too...if not for the sake of the friendship, then for overall morale in the house. "Unfortunately, it's not that easy."

"Ouch!" This exclamation Pam directed to her feet. She continued to knead furiously, as if she was working a loaf of bread dough. "So what's the problem?"

Gillian eyed her distrustfully. "You mean, Bridget didn't tell you?"

Pam just looked at her. "I'm asking *you*."

"Oh, it's dumb." Gillian wished they hadn't started this conversation. But Pam was waiting for an answer now, and she couldn't afford to alienate what might be her only remaining friend. She sighed. "You remember that guy in my department Bridget was interested in?"

"Yeah."

"Well, she's convinced that I like him, too, that's all. So she's mad."

"I see." Pam looked at her thoughtfully. "She's mad because she thinks you like him?"

"Uh-huh."

"Not because she thinks you aren't being honest with her?"

"No. I—" Gillian leaned one elbow against the arm of the couch. "You *have* been talking to Bridget," she said with a glare.

Pam dropped one aching dog to the floor and reached for its companion. "Look, Gillian. I'm not saying this to make you angry," she said, squeezing her big toe. "I promise you, Bridget isn't saying terrible things behind your back. She's just confused. She can't figure out why you won't tell her what you're really feeling."

"Maybe *I* don't know what I'm really feeling," groused Gillian.

"Maybe you don't," Pam said easily. She paused for a moment, then suggested, "And then again, maybe you do."

"You think I'm lying to Bridget?" Gillian opened her eyes wide. "And to you?"

"No." Pam shook her head calmly. "But I think you're trying pretty hard not to see something that's clear to everyone but you."

"Oh, great!" Gillian wailed. She threw her feet off the bright, overstuffed couch and planted them squarely on the almond-colored wool carpet beneath her. The subject she'd been avoiding for weeks could be put off no longer. "This is awful! What if I *do* like Max?"

"So what if you do?" Pam seemed unconcerned.

"So what? So *what?*" Gillian looked at her incredulously. "Do you have any idea what that would mean?"

Pam dropped her second foot to the floor. "Obviously not," she said dryly.

"Well, for one thing, there's *Keith*." Gillian waited for the wide-mouth "O" of realization that would follow, but Pam's expression remained blank.

"Right," she nodded. "So, what else?"

"What do you mean, what *else?*" Gillian continued to glare at her. "He's my boyfriend, for goodness' sake."

"I guess so." Reaching around to the back of her head, Pam pulled out several bobby pins, allowing her long, black hair to fall to her shoulders. "If you want to stretch the definition of the word."

"What's that supposed to mean?" There was warning in her voice.

"Gillian." Pam addressed her in the tone of one whose patience was being sorely tested. "You *never* talk about Keith. The two of you see each other only when it's convenient. When he goes out of town, it's like he doesn't even exist." She shook her head disapprovingly, as if that settled it. "Do you love him?"

"I don't know...." With elbows on her knees, Gillian dropped her head into her hands and held it there.

"Gil? Either you do or you don't." She waited only a second for her response. "Can you honestly say that you do?"

"Well...no." Once it was put that way, the answer was shockingly easy to give.

Pam gave a nod of satisfaction. "And does he love you?"

"Now, that I *don't* know."

"Well," she said thoughtfully, "I'd be surprised if he felt that strongly. Most guys know how to read the signs, and you haven't exactly been giving off love vibes."

"How do you know what kind of 'vibes' I give off? You're hardly ever around us," Gillian grumbled.

"True," her roommate admitted. "I stand corrected. I don't know what makes your relationship tick. But you do."

"Meaning?"

"Come on. Help me out here. Why are you dating Keith if you're not in love with him?"

Gillian lifted her chin from her hands. "Well...it's easy. There's no stress there, no pressure. Besides, I figured I might fall in love with him in time. You and Bridget seemed pretty sure that he's the one...."

"Gil, no one's saying you have to marry the guy," Pam told her matter-of-factly. "He's a sweetie, that's for sure. But that's all the more reason to let him off the hook, so he can find someone who will *really* love him."

Gillian felt even more confused than before. She'd never really thought that she was in love with Keith. So why did she feel disappointed now that Pam was telling her it was okay not to marry him. "But you always said—"

"I said that you should give him a *chance*. You've done that, I think. And I'm proud of you, Gillian. But you can't force love to happen, either, if it isn't there. At some point, you have to let go and move on."

"I thought the point was *not* to walk away from relationships."

"There's a balance. You just have to find it. There are some relationships that just don't work out. And that's okay." Pam absentmindedly fingered the bobby pins she held in one hand. "There are other relationships that are worth keeping." She looked at Gillian meaningfully. "Do you understand what I'm saying?"

"You're talking about Bridget." Pam wasn't telling her something she didn't already know. It was true that she hadn't been overly close to Bridget, by most people's standards. But nonetheless, Bridget was as good a friend to Gillian as anyone. "Honestly, I hate fighting with her. I really do. I'm just having a hard time getting past it. Part of me is angry because she just kept pushing me. She wouldn't leave me alone, you know?"

Pam inclined her chin in a brief acknowledgment. But although Gillian wanted to believe that her own feelings were justified, she knew that her behavior was not.

"I'm frustrated with myself, too, though," she admitted reluctantly. "I was pretty touchy about the whole subject. I wanted to pretend there wasn't a problem, but the whole time I knew there was a conflict inside me that wasn't going away. And there was Bridget, shoving the whole thing in my face. I guess I snapped. I didn't do it on purpose though. I *hate* the fact that I hurt her. Now I've got to find a way to make it up to her," she grumbled, "on top of everything else that's going on."

"You mean your feelings for Max?"

Gillian just stared at her hands.

"What *do* you feel for him, Gil?"

Gillian closed her eyes. She was tired of running, tired of hiding. Maybe it was about time she talked to *someone* about it. And Pam was perhaps the most trustworthy person she knew.

"There was a time when I absolutely adored him." She looked up with just a hint of an embarrassed smile. "I thought he was perfect. Then one day he walked out of my life, as suddenly as he had come into it." Unconsciously, one hand crept up to her mouth, and she started to gnaw nervously at one chipped nail. "I knew he hadn't done anything wrong, but I was angry with him just the same," she murmured.

"Because he left you?"

Gillian noticed the finger between her teeth and dropped her hand. "That was a big part of it," she said, blushing. "Maybe I was upset, too, because he didn't ever acknowledge how much I cared for him. On one hand, I would have felt humiliated if he knew I had a crush on him. But at the same time, I wanted him to care. He knew I liked him well enough, I suppose. I was a terrible tagalong," she laughed. "But sometimes, I still wonder if he had any idea how *much* I liked him. He couldn't have known I would keep thinking about him, nonstop, for two whole years. But it would have been nice if he'd just said, 'I know you're going to miss me, Gilly. I'm sorry I have to go.' Is that crazy?"

Pam shook her head. "There's nothing crazy about the way your heart feels. It may not always seem logical to the head, but the heart has its own reasons for the way it responds to people."

Gillian leaned back against the soft, bright-red sofa pillows and quietly reflected on Pam's words.

"Okay, so that's how you felt about Max back then," her friend broke in. "What about *now?*"

"Well...most of the time, I feel uncomfortable," Gillian confessed. "Sometimes I still feel angry. Every once in a while, I snap at him, for no reason at all. I can't imagine what he must think of me." After all the years of wanting Max to like her, she certainly wasn't helping her case any now.

"Do you have any idea how he feels about you?" Pam asked softly.

"I guess I have a good idea." She couldn't ignore the evidence, even if she wanted to. "I think he feels sort of brotherly toward me. Last week he told me he was worried about me. He thinks I'm alone in life." Gillian grabbed a loose throw pillow and held it in her lap. "I didn't agree with him at the time. But the more I think about it, the more I wonder if maybe he's right."

"Does he have any particular remedy in mind?" Pam's blue eyes twinkled mischievously. "Like *him,* maybe?"

"Please!" Gillian rolled her eyes heavenward. "No, it's not anything like that. Max says he thinks I have sort of a spiritual hole in my life. He believes that if I had a relationship with God, I'd have more *resources* to get me through the tough times." She plucked at the fabric she held between long suntanned fingers. "Do you think he's right, Pam?"

"I don't know," she said soberly. "The truth is, I'm not sure, myself, what to believe. But I *have* known some Christians who said that same thing Max did. They were good people. People I respected. I have to admit, I was kind of intrigued."

"Yeah," Gillian said thoughtfully. "I am, too."

Pam leaned forward and peered at her intently. "It sounds like this guy really likes you, Gil, if he cared enough to worry about you like that."

"You think?" The words came out sounding more hopeful than she had intended.

"Yeah," Pam said with a knowing smirk. "*I think.* And you know what else I think?" Gillian had her suspicions, but she shook her head. "I think Bridget's right. I think you like him, too."

Out of habit, Gillian started to shake her head, then stopped herself and grinned like a fool. The truth was out. There was no hiding it.

For better or worse, she was gloriously, deliriously, and completely smitten with Max Bishop.

Again.

Nine

And the LORD God formed the man from the dust of the ground....
GENESIS 2:7

July 27, 1987

From the first moment he met Max, my father should have realized that he had met his match. His favorite students have always been the ones who swallowed his theories whole, like seals clapping for fish. But Max isn't that easy. There are too many questions wrapped up inside him. I knew it all along. I could see it in Max's eyes. Dad could have seen it too, if he'd just been paying attention.

I've said that I wished I could forget all about Max. I don't suppose that was ever likely, but after what happened last night, there's not even a chance of it.

It started out as one of those rare times when Dad, Mom, and I actually were acting like a regular family. All week the weather had been pretty steamy. Mom hates being all hot and sticky, so she set up a cheap plastic sprinkler in the backyard and planted her blue-and-white patio chair just beyond the water's arc. From there she could just barely reach one scarlet-colored toenail out into the spray, or just lay back and enjoy the traces of mist that drifted by.

Well, I'm no dummy, and neither is Dad. Hot is hot, and it was pretty clear right then who was the real brain in the family. Pretty soon we had our chairs out there in a small semicircle of three, with mine smack-dab in the middle. Very "Father Knows Best."

We'd been out there for about twenty minutes when Max showed up. Dad must have been expecting him, although I hadn't heard anything about it beforehand, and I'm usually pretty good about keeping up on Max and Dad's schedule. Since the whole mess up with Jenny, though, I guess I've been pretty out of it.

Anyway, my family was gathered around the sprinkler like it was some crazy campfire or something, and Mom was telling Dad and me stories about which political candidate was under indictment for taking bribes and which was spending the summer letting his hair plugs heal. When Max got there, Dad didn't get up right away—I guess the heat was getting to him, too—and I finally got to just sit back and watch Max up close.

For a while, he and my dad chatted about critical density, special and general relativity, kinetic energy. You know, the usual stuff. After a while, Dad asked Max if he had decided on a subject for his first big paper of the fall. Max said that he had. Everything was still fine at that point. But when Max told him what he'd chosen as his topic, I thought my father was going to have some sort of fit, right there under the sprinkler.

"You propose to reconcile evidence supporting the big bang theory with the theological teachings in Genesis?" Veins bulged at the side of Dad's neck. The sprinkler wasn't much help any more. He was getting hotter by the second. "That's not science, Bishop. That's fiction!"

"I disagree, sir," Max said respectfully. "And I'm going to prove it in my paper."

My mom charged right in. "You don't actually expect to give religious credence to that…that theory?" I think she liked the idea of arguing science and religion without attacking my father directly—every time she disagreed with him about it, they ended up fighting. Poor Max was the lamb, and Mom was ready for the slaughter. "The Bible clearly states that God made the earth in six days," she said primly. "I understand that according to the big bang theory, it would have taken at least four-and-a-half billion years to create the earth, and maybe fifteen billion years or more to create the universe." I stared at her. She might not agree with Dad's beliefs, but at least she was listening to him. The woman knew her facts.

"That's right," Max answered cheerfully enough.

"But you're saying you plan to reconcile these two theories." She, too, looked at him as if he was crazy. "What's the compromise?"

"Oh, there's no compromise, Mrs. Spencer," Max reassured her. "The creation of the universe took ten to twenty billion years, all right. But it's also true that it took six days."

Dad sat silently, working his jaw like a cow chewing its cud. Mom didn't even blink. Max just smiled back at them, while I watched all three to see who would move first.

Mom was the one who broke the spell. After several long seconds, she sat up and peered closely at Max, like he was a magician and she was determined to figure out where he'd hidden the rabbit. Suddenly, she had an insight. You could almost see the light bulb appear over her head. "Oh, I see!" she said smugly and leaned back again in her chair. "You're not a literalist, then. You're one of those people who believes that the Genesis account is a metaphor. Each 'day' equals six billion years.…"

"Oh no," Max broke in. "It was a literal six days. Six twenty-four-hour days," he assured her. By this time, Dad was on the edge of his rickety patio chair, veins bulging bigger with every word. Any minute, I figured, he was gonna fall right off.

"Are you trying to tell me that both explanations can be true?" Mom obviously thought Max was some kind of heretic. It didn't seem to bother him a bit.

"I believe that they not only can be…they are," he said confidently.

"All right, young man." Mom took it upon herself to issue the challenge. "You'd better explain. And be very careful." She threw Dad a sideways glance and laughed. "The master is watching."

"Well...I haven't really articulated my thoughts yet, but I have an idea of where I'm going with the subject for my paper...." For a second, Max looked a little uncertain, like he wasn't quite prepared to go down that road yet. He stopped for a moment and seemed to be considering his approach. "Okay," he said finally. "Let's start with the basics. What we're looking at here are two different premises: First, the scientific theory that the universe was created over a period of ten to twenty billion years. This hypothesis is supported by measured scientific evidence, including paleontological discoveries, carbon dating, and the observed behavior of light waves. Next, there's your second theory: That the universe was created in six days by an omnipotent being. This theory is supported primarily by religious tradition and scriptural accounts inspired by divine revelation." Max held his hands out, palms upturned, presenting himself as a human scale. "Both theories pretty hard to argue with," he said diplomatically. His expression was cool, impassive. He was the very picture of objectivity.

"At first the two theories seem so mutually exclusive, it's tempting to choose one over the other or to ignore the problem completely and pretend it doesn't exist. Wouldn't you say?"

"Yeah," I agreed. Mom and Dad both turned and looked at me. I'd never expressed any interest in the subject before. But they'd never explained it this way before. Max spoke as if it was a mystery to be solved, not a battle to be won.

"So, Mrs. Spencer, let's look a little more closely at the problem." Max lowered one hand and laid it open in front of him, as if presenting evidence for examination. "The amount of time that passes during the period of creation described in the first few verses of the Bible is completely inconsistent with time measured on earth. Does this problem occur concerning any other verses in the Bible?"

"Well...no. Not that I'm aware of."

"That's my understanding, too. The time discrepancy applies only to the days of creation before God rested. So we're looking at, what? Six days? What happens on the sixth day?"

"God made man," Mom supplied, ever the dutiful Bible student.

"Right." Max's head bobbed up and down. "So, is it true, would you say, that before the sixth day, there were no humans around to measure time? Just...God?"

Dad made a face like a man being tortured, but I could see that Mom was really getting into what Max was saying. I have to admit...I was, too.

"I suppose so," Mom said.

"Okay, now, Gilly. Let's pull you into this. What do you know about Einstein's special and general theories of relativity?"

The sun was going down, but I started to sweat even more. "Well, $E=mc^2$ states that the energy of a photon equals —"

"No, no. Forget the formulas. Tell me what the theories mean."

My mouth felt as dry as sand. I swallowed hard. Dad was watching me real close, and I didn't want to botch it up. "Basically, Einstein's theories state that the passage of time for an observer, traveling near the speed of light, is relative."

Max nodded. "How does this affect the passage of time?"

"Well I guess it means it's possible for two people in two different places to measure the same exact event in completely different time frames. Each frame is different, yet completely true and accurate for the person from whose perspective the event is measured."

Max beamed at me like he was the professor and I was his star pupil. Mom looked a little surprised. But, Dad...Dad looked like his tongue was about to drop out of his mouth. I almost laughed. He had no idea I knew all this stuff. But...please. I'm no dummy. I've taken physics. Besides, you can't be a kid in Dr. Joseph Spencer's house and grow up not knowing something about quantum cosmology. See, I'd been listening, too.

Max turned back to my mom. "Do you understand now, Mrs. Spencer, what I'm getting at?"

"I—I think so," she said slowly. "You're saying that it's possible for man and God to be looking at the event from two different time frames? At the same time?"

"That's what I believe."

I hadn't thought of that before. I didn't know what else to say.

"But aren't Einstein's theories just...well, theories?" Mom asked timidly. With my dad nearby, she knew she was treading on dangerous ground. "It's not as if they've been proven true."

Dad rolled his eyes and turned a darker shade of red. The veins kept bulging. But Max responded kindly to Mom, just like he always did to me.

"Actually, they have," he explained. "The word theory can be a little bit misleading. Einstein's discoveries have been proven to be scientifically accurate." Mom blushed. "Don't feel bad, though," Max told her. "Not everyone knows that. It's pretty common for people to 'tune out' when someone talks about Einstein's teachings. Taken as a whole, they can be pretty overwhelming. But the basic principles behind them are pretty understandable."

"And you're saying that these principles are the answer to the stand-off between religion and science?"

"I'm saying there doesn't have to be a stand-off," Max said simply. "What we're talking about here is a very real, scientifically proven phenomenon called relativistic time dilation—a phenomenon that completely allows for a biblical, six-day creation of the universe."

"This is ridiculous," Dad muttered. I looked at him in surprise. He'd been quiet for so long, I'd almost forgotten he was there. I would have thought the debate would have stirred him up, but he didn't look like he wanted to argue, particularly. He just looked disgusted. He shook his head. "There is no scientific evidence that suggests that there is any god who made the world—either in six days or in billions of years. There are clearer, more rational explanations for how the universe began."

Okay, I decided. I'll bite. "Like what?"

Dad turned on me. "Haven't you ever heard of 'singularity'?" *I nodded. I had. But he wasn't looking at me anymore. His focus was solely on Mom now.* "Scientific study has led physicists to an understanding of singularity, a phenomenon in which matter is compressed into a single point where the gravitational field and the density of matter are infinite," *he told her.* "Today, scientists believe that the universe once existed in such a state of singularity. This highly dense, and infinitely small compressed point contained all galaxies, all radiation, all matter." *Dad was sitting up in his chaise lounge now, with his feet planted firmly on the misty ground, and his legs buckled awkwardly at either side of the chair. The expression on his face was intense. He was getting into it now, too.*

"At some time, this point exploded, sending galaxies spinning into the outer reaches of the universe, which continued to expand—and are still expanding today," *he explained, as if this were a fact known and accepted by everyone who had even a shred of intelligence. Mom looked at Max, as though she suspected she couldn't trust Dad. I think she expected Max to jump in and save her, but he just nodded. Mom looked unpleasantly surprised. She had always pooh-poohed Dad's passing comments about the big bang theory. I could tell it bothered her that Max wasn't arguing with him. For a moment or two, words escaped her.*

"And you think that this negates any evidence that might point toward a creator?" *She finally gave in and asked my father.*

"Of course I do," *Dad grumbled, as if it should be obvious.*

"Sir, I respectfully disagree," *Max interrupted. Dad's jaw dropped, just a fraction. My hero! I almost cheered. The day was shaping up pretty great after all.*

"What about all evidence to the contrary? What about evolution?" *Dad glared at him.*

Max just looked right back. "I'm not convinced."

"You must be joking!" *Dad was appalled.* "There is clear evidence that, over time, simple forms of life have developed into more complex forms."

Max shook his head. "I'm not sure it's as clear as you believe."

"You can't dispute all the evidence of evolution—?"

"Evidence of microevolution doesn't prove macroevolution," Max said evenly. "The development of various species over time doesn't justify the theory that man developed from lower forms of life. There's still no evidence of a 'missing link.' The theory you're talking about requires a greater leap of faith than that demanded of those who support a creationist theory."

"I still don't get it," I heard myself saying. I almost jumped in surprise. I hadn't intended to say a word.

"What don't you get, Gilly?" Max asked, turning his full attention on me.

"Well, you're saying that six days can equal fifteen billion years or more. But that's not the only problem, is it? In school, I learned that the building blocks needed for life started at the big bang. But the Bible says God made man from dust. Just, like, from out of thin air."

"It doesn't say anything about thin air, Gilly," Max corrected me gently but firmly. "That's just our simple human perception. Let's think about this for a minute. What if just maybe the things your mom and dad believe are both true?"

Now I was the one looking at him like he was a lunatic. "Right. How's that possible?"

"What your father believes—and correct me if I'm wrong, sir— is what many other scientists believe: that the earth is made of matter that was once supercompressed through the birth, life, death, and rebirth of countless stars. This process gave us the building blocks for life."

Dad nodded, grudgingly.

"See, that's not what the Bible says at all," I said.

"Does the Bible say exactly how God made the universe, Gilly? What the process was?"

I thought back to everything my mom had tried to teach me. "Well...no. Not that I know of."

"And if Einstein's teachings are true—and we know that they are—then isn't it possible that God could have pulled the material he needed for the earth from that material that once came from other stars?"

"I suppose."

"Okay, then. The Bible doesn't say exactly how God made the universe. Or mankind. You have to form your own opinion, Gilly. But you know what I think? I think it's entirely possible that God did it exactly the way your dad says it happened. God's not an illusionist. He's a creator. He made us from something. Maybe even elements on earth that originally came from stars." He looked deep into my eyes. And suddenly, I wasn't thinking about how cute he was. I was thinking about how much sense he was making. And how much I wanted to be like him.

He leaned forward and whispered, as if sharing a great secret. "Maybe, Gilly, just maybe...you and I are both made of stardust."

And the way his eyes twinkled, just like the stars, I knew it must be true.

July 23, 1997

Warm beams of golden light poured through the white-trimmed windowpanes, teasing Gillian with just a taste of summer sun. On either side of her, at the kitchen table, piles of file folders and stacks of thick, dusty tomes obscured the cheerful blue-and-white tablecloth. Gillian stared dolefully at the mess around her. She hated working on the weekend...hated wasting a perfectly good Saturday morning most of all. But with her heavy load, and with her half-time class schedule, there was no avoiding it. At least she could ease the pain of the situation by curling up in her favorite corner of the old country farmhouse.

The sound of footsteps padding down the hall offered a much-needed distraction.

"Hey, Pam?" she called. "What are you doing up so early? I thought you stayed up late last night making—" Her voice broke off at the sight of the curly brown head that appeared in the doorway. She hadn't seen Bridget in several days; she hadn't even considered that it might be her approaching. "Oh, hi." Gillian tried to keep her voice friendly, but it wasn't easy. She disliked stressful situations, and this was one of the toughest she had experienced in a long time. "How's it going?"

Bridget averted her gaze and made a beeline for the refrigerator. "Okay, I guess," she said, her head disappearing behind the appliance's enormous white door.

Feeling snubbed, Gillian, in turn, buried her nose in the book that was open on the table before her. If Bridget didn't want to talk, then they wouldn't talk. Two could play at that game.

She stopped reading as the thought sank in. A game? *A game?* This wasn't supposed to be a game. She and Bridget were both grown-ups. They were friends...more or less. There wasn't any reason why they shouldn't be able to work through this. Especially if *someone* were to take a step forward and apologize...

Instinctively, Gillian knew that person had to be her. She cringed at the thought.

It isn't as though I hurt Bridget on purpose, she thought defensively. *And it's not like Bridget didn't hurt me, too. It wasn't very nice of her to push me, the way she did.* The more Gillian thought about it, the angrier she got. *It isn't anyone's business but my own who I like or don't like. If I want to keep that information to myself—or even if I'm not ready to face the situation yet—that's my prerogative. Bridget had no right—no right at all—to insist that I...*

"Gillian, did you eat my last egg? It was in here yesterday."

The accusation caught Gillian off guard, and she struggled to keep the cutting edge from her tone. "Nope. But I saw Pam mixing some eggs into a batch of cookie dough last night," Gillian told her. "Maybe she thought it was one of hers." Bridget stuck her nose around the refrigerator door and looked at Gillian, as though she wasn't sure whether or not to believe her. After a moment's consideration, she resumed her silent inventory of the refrigerator's contents.

Gillian fumed. *See? What is that all about? Here I am, being perfectly civil, and she automatically assumes that I'm the one who took her crummy ol' egg. That shows how much she trusts me. Probably about as much as I trust her....*

Gillian laid down the volume she held in her hands and considered the matter further. It was true. She *didn't* trust Bridget. Not enough to lay herself open and ask for forgiveness...even though she knew full well that she had been just as insensitive as—if not *more* insensitive than—Bridget had been. It was a shame, because if one of them didn't take steps toward repairing their broken relationship—and soon—the damage to their friendship could become permanent. She really wasn't looking forward to beginning the roommate search again. Over and over, the cycle ran...a new roommate, some sort of conflict, time to move on.... If she was going to have to go through such struggles, why not go through it with Bridget and work things out?

Across the room, Bridget had abandoned her egg quest and was instead placing a filter full of coffee grounds inside her kitschy old Mr. Coffee machine. Gillian pondered the situation. Her roommate wasn't going anywhere. Bridget would have to wait for the drink to brew. There would be no better opportunity to say what she had to say.

"Umm...Bridget?" The words rushed quickly off her tongue before she had a chance to change her mind.

"Yeah?" Bridget put her hands behind her back and rested them against the white Formica kitchen counter, then leaned against them, appearing casual.

"I...uh, I've been thinking." Gillian licked her lips nervously. "About what you said the other night, and...well, you're right. I haven't been completely honest with you. Or myself."

Bridget opened her brown eyes wide at the confession. "You haven't." It was a confirmation, not a question.

"No. I've been examining my feelings, and I—" She took a deep breath. The words were as difficult to say as she had feared. "I think I may still feel...*something* for Max after all these years."

"Oh." Bridget's bright eyes clouded over. It was clear that she liked him, too. Gillian's heart went out to her. "Have you told this to Max?" Bridget asked weakly.

"No!" Shocked by the question, Gillian nearly yelped out her response. She cleared her throat and said, more evenly, "And I'm not going to, either. I don't actually want to *date* him. I just have some unresolved issues that need to be dealt with—"

Bridget turned away in disgust. "Gillian, you're doing it again." She leaned down and watched the dark liquid dripping into the pot.

"What do you mean?" Gillian protested. "All I said was—" Her eyes flickered back and forth as she analyzed her response. "Oh, all *right,*" she admitted with a groan. "Part of me really would like to date him, just like before. But that doesn't mean I'm actually *going* to." The thought was ridiculous. He didn't like her as anything but a friend. She couldn't believe they were even discussing it. "I couldn't go, even if he asked. Which he *won't*. I've got a boyfriend, you know."

"I know," Bridget said coolly. "Which reminds me...have you talked to *Keith* about this?" She reached up into the cupboard and withdrew her favorite blue ceramic mug.

"No, there really isn't any point."

Bridget gripped the handle of the coffeepot and began to pour into the enormous cup. "Of course there is," she said, reaching for the sugar bowl with her free hand. "You've got feelings for another man. Don't you think that will have an effect on your relationship with Keith?"

In her mind, Gillian wasn't sure that it would. "I don't know. We've never been very territorial—"

"Gillian! For goodness' sake, you two aren't wolves." Bridget made a face as she spooned the white crystals into her mug. "Do you *plan* to talk to Keith about it, at least?"

Gillian squirmed under the examination. "I...don't know. Not yet, anyway. Not until I know what I feel—"

"Well, *I* know what you feel, and I think Keith has a right to know, too." Bridget set her mouth in a hard line. Her spoon clattered against the countertop, where she dropped it.

"What are you saying?"

"Just that...maybe I'll tell Keith, if you won't."

"Bridget!" Surely she was kidding. Gillian could almost feel her blood pressure rising. "You wouldn't do that!"

"Men aren't toys, you know. You can't just play with them."

"But I'm not—"

"I'm serious, Gillian!" Bridget paced the vinyl floor. "I still see Max around the campus. He hasn't asked me out once, but he stops and talks to me about you. He's got a thing for you. You must know that."

Gillian didn't know any such thing, but it was clear that Bridget believed it.

"I know I sound jealous." Bridget's voice quivered as she spoke. "I don't mean to. But I can't help it. And I know it's selfish and mean-spirited of me, but I can't help feeling angry and well...sort of betrayed." The cup in her hand shook a little, and she looked as if she might cry. "It's not that you don't have a right to like Max," she said unhappily. "It's just that you acted like you were on my side, when you really weren't. You led me on, made me think you'd set me up with him. You got my hopes up, then you cut me down by telling me not to believe that he might like me. And then you lied to me about how you felt about him yourself."

Each word was like a poison dart and this time Gillian felt every sting.

"Bridget, you're right. I wasn't being a very good friend," she said awkwardly. If there was a way to make things right, she wanted to do it. At the same time, she feared promising too much. She wanted to be a good friend, but she had somehow always managed to fall short of the mark. Bridget didn't want her to lie anymore. Was it a lie to promise that she wouldn't hurt her again? That she wouldn't fail?

"I don't know what to tell you, except that I didn't do it on purpose," she said quietly. "I thought I was okay about him coming back. I wanted *not* to like him. Then, when I realized the way things were going, I didn't know how to deal with you—" Bridget looked at her miserably, as if Gillian had just accused her of something terrible. "Oh no, Bridget! That's not what I mean. It wasn't your fault, wasn't because of anything *you'd* done. I know I'm responsible for my own feelings. It's just really hard for me to let people get close to me." She tried to think of some way to explain. "You know how we've always kidded about me losing all my boyfriends 'cause I won't give them a chance? I never saw that I was holding my friends at arm's length, too."

Her eyes cried out for Bridget to understand. "I'm sorry. Really I am. And from now on, I'm going to *try* at least to do the right thing." That, at least, seemed like a fairly safe promise.

"If you want to do the right thing, I suggest you talk with

Keith." Bridget still sounded hesitant to trust her.

Gillian stared out the window at the brilliant morning light. "I suppose you're right," she said with a sigh. It was time to act responsibly. It was time to face what she'd been running from for so long. "I'm supposed to see him tomorrow night. I'll talk to him then." She turned to look out the window to her left. A cloud passed over the sun, obscuring it's golden face. And suddenly the day seemed darker...in more ways than one.

Ten

*The human heart is like a ship on a stormy sea, driven about
by winds blowing from all four corners of heaven.*
MARTIN LUTHER, PREFACE TO HIS TRANSLATION
OF THE PSALMS, 1534

August 2, 1987

*I was riding my bike hard today—my hair whipping in the wind like
some ridiculous scarf—the way I always do when I'm upset. Mom
worries about me when I'm like this, and I guess she's got a point. I
don't pay a lot of attention to what's going on around me when I'm
angry. I suppose that's why I didn't see the Bug until I had almost hit it.*

*I'm not talking about getting a bug caught in my teeth, although
when I ride all wild like this, that happens, too. I'm talking about the
beat-up old 1967 Volkswagen Beetle, white, except for one pitiful-
looking red fender. I know that Bug like I know my own bike, so
you'd think I would have noticed. But I didn't...not before I was
almost under it.*

*I was heading east on Route 518, almost to the quarry, and had
just raised myself up to a standing position to push on the pedals, as
hard as I could—it's a major hill. Even though I was putting all my
weight into it, I could barely keep the bike moving. I grunted. I
wheezed. But I refused to give up. I kept my eyes on my feet, and I
guess I was looking down longer than I realized 'cause before I knew
it, I had drifted over the center line and was headed into the opposite
lane.*

I didn't know it, though, until I heard a sick little cry that sounded like a bleating sheep that was actually the Volkswagen's horn. I looked up and there it was, heading down the hill, right at me. I gave a little scream and cranked the handlebars hard to the right, veering back over to my side and crashing along the roadside.

My arms and legs stung like anything, but I have to say it's the humiliation that hurt the worst. I untangled myself from the wreckage of my bike and looked back over my shoulder. Sure enough, he was on his way over. I was picking black, hard pieces of gravel out of my knee when he got to me.

"Gilly, what on earth? Are you okay?" Max knelt down beside me to help.

"Yeah..." I told him, keeping my eyes lowered. I'd never been so embarrassed in all my life.

"But...what were you doing? Don't you know you could have gotten killed?" His breath came in short gasps. "If you'd been any closer to the top of the hill, I wouldn't have had time to stop! I would have...I..." For a second, Max looked as though he was going to cry. I guess I did, too, because then he grabbed my hands and held them tight. "Kiddo...you scared me to death." He let go of one hand, put a finger under my chin, and turned it gently so I had no choice but to face him.

I finally met his look then, and my own eyes filled up with tears. I think my lower lip trembled, the traitor. "I'm sorry, Max. I didn't mean to. I guess I just wasn't thinking." I tried to sound natural, but my voice was all tight and strained from trying not to cry. It was too late to stop it, though. I could read the emotions on his face—concern, relief, and something else, something sort of protective. I don't remember anyone else ever looking at me like that before. It was more than I could take. Within a few seconds, I was bawling.

Max hesitated, just for a second, then placed his arms around my shaking shoulders. You'd think I would have enjoyed the moment. How long have I been dreaming about Max putting his arms around me? But all I could do was sob. I was completely out of control. I felt my eyes puff up, the way they always do when I cry, and pretty soon my nose was making all sorts of disgusting noises. Max dug into his pocket and pulled out a couple of lint-covered paper napkins from some fast-food place. He laid one of them against the bloodiest of my knees. The second, he handed to me. Feeling like a fool, I put it to my nose and blew...hard.

Dainty, I am not. At the foghornlike sound, both Max and I laughed. "Wow," he said. "If I'd had a horn like that, maybe you could have gotten out of the way quicker."

"Unh-unh." I shook my head and wiped at the dirt that was ground into my skinned palms. "If you'd had a horn like that, you would have scared me right off my bike. I never would have had a chance."

Max laughed, a strong, hearty laugh that made me wish I laughed more, too. "Let me see that," he said, reaching for my left hand. He bent down and inspected it closely, then the right. After doing the same with my knees, he told me that he thought I would live.

"But just to be on the safe side," he said, "why don't you let me drive you home?"

"Thanks." That was a relief. The way my knees were stinging, I wasn't looking forward one bit to biking home. "Mom always warns me not to ride when I'm mad. I guess she was right."

Max climbed to his feet, then helped me to mine. I reached for my bike, but he nudged me away, telling me to just keep the napkin pressed to my knee. In just a few minutes, he had the bike strapped to the back of the Bug and was helping me into the passenger seat.

"So...what's all this about you being mad?" he asked as he climbed in the driver's side. "What's on your mind?"

"Oh...it's nothing," I told him. I'd already humiliated myself enough. I figured he didn't really want to hear about my problems.

But apparently he did, because he kept pushing—in a nice way.

"You know, when I'm having a hard time with something, it usually helps me to talk to a friend about it." He jammed his key into the ignition and cranked it, causing the Bug to sputter and shake. "I think you and I are friends, don't you, Gilly?"

I really didn't know what to say to that. Max considers me his friend? "I hope so." I tried to say it coolly, but I sounded all soft and breathless, like the lovesick teenager I am. "I mean, I'd like—"

The corners of Max's mouth crinkled up. He didn't look embarrassed at all. "So, shoot. Tell me what's on your mind."

I sighed. "Oh, it's just Mom and Dad. They got in a big fight this morning. Norrie's taking vacation next week, and Mom's going off to Washington. She was counting on Dad to keep an eye on me, but he just told her at the last minute that he's getting an award at some ceremony in Tucson. So now, either Mom has to cancel, or I'm going to be on my own." I turned to him and spoke very clearly, making sure he heard every word. "It's not a big deal to me. I mean, I'm sixteen years old you know." It was important that he realize I did not need a baby-sitter. "Sixteen."

"I know," he said, and let it go at that.

I leaned my head against the glass and watched the road signs pass. "I just hate it when they fight, that's all," I said. I didn't bother to tell him how often it happened. He didn't need to know what a mess my family really was.

"Well, I don't know exactly what to tell you, Gilly," he said as we turned into my driveway. My heart sank at the sight of our house and yard. Time with Max is what I live for, practically. I hated for it to be over. "I don't know the specifics of the situation," he went on, "and I don't really need to. But I do know that a lot of parents fight. You're not alone there."

Max maneuvered the Volkswagen around Mom's silver Volvo and turned the engine off. The Bug sighed and sputtered into silence. He put one arm across the headrest behind me, but without touching me even a little bit. "I imagine you must feel really bad right now. Tell you what." I hoped maybe he'd reach out and take my hand again, like he had along the roadside, but he didn't. "I talk to a lot of friends about my problems, but one friend most of all: I talk to God when things are bothering me. If you'd like, I'll talk to him about you, too.."

Coming from anyone else, it might have sounded weird. But I could tell by the look on his face that he wanted to help me, and I guess this was the nicest thing he could think of to do.

"O-okay," I said. I wasn't sure I actually wanted him to pray for me, but it was really comforting to know that someone cared. "That would be nice."

Max climbed out of the Bug, and I did the same. We spent the next few minutes examining my bike. Thank goodness, there was no major damage, only a few dings and scrapes—just like on me.

"All right, Evel Knievel," he said with a grin and then began heading back toward Dad's office. "Stay on your side of the road, now. And remember," he threw the words over his shoulder, "I'll be thinking of you."

"Yeah," I whispered, but so he couldn't hear me. "I'll be thinking of you, too."

August 2, 1997

"So then, I had to go before Judge Linwood, who, of course, I had run into that afternoon with his *girlfriend*." With a triumphant stab of his knife, Keith pierced the last bit of herbed salmon steak that lay before him. "He looked at me over the bench, our eyes met...and I knew I had him. There was no way he was going to risk letting his wife find out. Of course, I'd *never* get involved in something like that, but he didn't know that for sure. I could have *sneezed* my way through the entire cross-examination and still, he would have..."

With slow, careless strokes, Gillian dragged her fork through the mess on her plate. Once a beautiful dish of fresh, warm penne pasta, the mixture before her was now cold and unappetizing.

Bits of pale salmon and dark spices peeked out at her from the heavy, quickly solidifying cream sauce. Normally she would have devoured every bite. The Peacock Inn was her favorite restaurant, and their signature dish—lobster in a port wine sauce, served outside the shell but rearranged on the plate as a full lobster—was her favorite meal. Tonight, however, everything tasted flat. Even the water.

Across the table, Keith continued to chatter on about his day in court. Occasionally, Gillian nodded or displayed some other sign of interest, but for the most part, she let her mind wander.

"If you want to do the right thing...talk with Keith," Bridget had said. Ever since she'd spoken the words, Gillian had been dreading this moment. If she could have put it off any longer, she would have. But the most frustrating thing about Bridget's words was that she was horribly right. Gillian wasn't actively participating in her relationship any longer...and Keith had a right to know the reason why.

"Gil? Are you listening?" A lock of white-blond hair fell across Keith's eyes, making him look much younger than his thirty-three years.

"Hmm?" Gillian's fork fell to her plate with a clatter. "What? Oh, sorry, Keith. My mind was just—" She gave him a rueful grin. "Sorry."

"Are you okay?" He popped the last bit of steak into his mouth.

"Sure I am." Gillian smiled brightly and picked up her fork again. "Honest. Now, what were you saying?"

Caught with his mouth full, Keith made a face and started chewing harder. Once he had swallowed his bite, he took a long drink of lemon water before repeating himself. "I asked you if you'd be interested in heading up to New York next weekend to visit my folks. My cousin Vince is heading in from

Detroit, and I promised I'd go and see him."

"Next weekend, huh?" Keith was great, but Gillian had no desire to go spend three days with his family. "I—I don't think so, Keith. I'm just so swamped. I really think I need to work."

"Even on the weekend?" He looked appalled. "You're sure working a lot these days, Gillian. Are you sure it's good for you? I don't know if it's a good idea to let this Max guy put so much pressure on you."

She shrugged it off and picked at the green beans on her plate. "Oh, it's okay, Keith. Really. I enjoy it."

"You enjoy getting pushed around?"

Gillian looked up in surprise. It wasn't like Keith to voice an opinion so strongly. That was one of the things she liked best about their relationship: he always gave her the space she needed.

"It's a great project," she said firmly, then added, "I enjoy working with Max." There. It was out. And as good a time as any to broach the subject she'd been avoiding. "Um, Keith?" Gillian tried to get his attention, but he was focused completely on their waitress, trying to flag her down with his eyes. "I was thinking about...that is, I've been feeling..." Oh, phooey. This wasn't going well at all.

"Oh, Miss?" Keith called out. The woman turned on one thin black heel and made a beeline for him. Gillian was amazed. The man drew women like flies.

He held up his cup, offering his unspoken request. Gillian watched as the woman threw Keith a flirtatious little smile, then leaned close to him as she poured his coffee. She didn't even have the decency to look apologetic when Gillian caught her eye.

"Gil?" Gillian turned to see his eyes were back on her. "You were saying?" he supplied.

She pushed all thoughts about the waitress from her mind.

"Sorry. It's just that there's something that's been bothering me. I don't *want* to talk about it...but I feel like I *have* to."

The expression that flickered across his face could, oddly enough, almost be described as one of pleasure.

"Sure, Gillian. I'd like very much to know what's going on."

"Okay, well...this isn't easy to say. I don't know of any other way to do it than to just tell you." She took a deep breath and squeezed the napkin in her lap. "Remember when I told you that Max had been a student of my father's?"

Keith nodded calmly, but the look of pleasure faded slightly.

Gillian swallowed hard. "Well, at the time I had a huge crush on him. That was ten years ago. I didn't think much of it when he first came back, but after I started working with him...well, a lot of those old feelings came back."

Keith's eyes widened in dawning understanding. "I...see. You want to break up with me so you can date Max."

"No!" Normally, she was not one given to public displays of affection. But now, Gillian reached out to grab his hand and held it tight. "Oh no. That's not it at all. I don't want to break up! I just want to talk about what's going on inside. I feel like I've been hiding something from you, and I just wanted to be truthful."

Keith listened to her words, but his hand lay still and unresponsive against hers.

Gillian's heart started beating faster. "Honest, Keith," she said a little desperately. "*Nothing* has happened between Max and me, and it's not going to. This isn't about what's happening today or tomorrow. It's about my past and the unresolved feelings I thought I'd left there." She closed her eyes and uttered a brief prayer to the God she wasn't sure she believed in. *Oh, Lord. Please help me out of this one....* Why on earth had she listened to Bridget?

"Are you sure you wouldn't rather date Max?" Keith asked heavily.

"*No.* I mean—yes!" Gillian struggled to regain her composure. "That is, I'm dating *you.*"

"I realize that." The way he said the words, it didn't sound like a good thing. "Do you love him?"

"What!" Gillian's eyes narrowed. "Love Max? Are you kidding? I'm not even going out with him."

"That's not the point. I'm asking if you love him."

She scrambled for an honest answer. "Max has been like...like a big brother to me. Of course I love him, in *that* sense."

"But are you *in love* with him?"

"Keith, don't be silly!" Things were getting completely out of hand. "For one thing, Max barely knows I'm alive. He certainly isn't in love with me...."

"I'm not asking about his feelings. I'm asking about *yours.* Come on, Gillian. Please. Answer the question."

"I—" More than anything, Gillian wanted to deny it. But the way Keith was looking at her, she knew she couldn't give him anything but the truth. "I—have a crush on him, I suppose. Just like I did as a kid. Is that what you mean? Is that love?"

"Sometimes," Keith said thoughtfully. "Sometimes not." He searched her face carefully. "I think you know in your heart what you feel for him, Gillian. Maybe you're not aware of the truth yet. But I think you owe it to yourself to find it." There was an air of finality to his tone.

"What are you saying?" Gillian suddenly felt slightly dizzy. "Is this it? Are you breaking up with me?"

Keith stared at his hands for a moment, not moving. Then he answered, "Gillian, it's not just Max. You and I have had problems for a long time."

The words stunned her. "We have?"

"Yes," Keith said evenly. "We have. The truth is, I've been thinking a lot lately about our relationship, and I haven't been

145

so sure that we should stick with it."

Gillian stared at him, her hazel eyes wide. "But why?"

"Because you just don't trust me, Gillian," he said simply. "We never talk about anything serious. Just our work, our shared interests...nothing really about what's going on inside our hearts."

"But I thought we both liked it that way!"

"No, Gillian." Keith's voice was heavy. "*You* liked it that way. You rarely show any interest in getting to know me better. And when I ask you personal questions, you change the subject before I even know what's happened. Our relationship works on a surface level, but not a deep one," he said sadly. "For a minute there, when you said you wanted to talk, I thought there might be a chance after all. But now that I think about it, I'm certain this is the right decision."

Gillian felt a sudden hollowness in her chest. "I didn't bring this up so we'd split up!" she wailed.

"I know you didn't," Keith said gently. "But I think if you search your heart, you'll agree that it's the best thing for us."

"But I don't *want* to be in love with Max!"

"Why not?"

"Because..."

"Yes?"

"Because...he hurt me."

Keith nodded. "How did he do that?"

"I don't know." Gillian sounded like a pouty child. "He just...left, that's all."

"Did you feel that he should have stayed?"

Her head was spinning. Was this twenty questions? "No. Of course not."

"Then, what were you angry about?"

Gillian let out a loud sigh and glared at him in frustration. "I wasn't angry at Max. I was angry at *me*," she said. "For being so dumb! For loving him. For...for laying my heart out there to get trampled on." Even as she spoke the words, Gillian felt a tightness growing inside her chest.

"Gillian..." Keith kept his voice low and calming. "Was that the first time you felt that way? Was there anyone else you loved who trampled on your heart?"

"Are you kidding?" she laughed bitterly. "I don't remember loving anyone who *didn't* trample on it."

"When was the last time you felt that way? When was the last time you lost someone you truly loved?"

She thought for a moment. "I guess...when Max left."

Keith sat back in his chair and folded his arms. "Look, Gillian. I don't want to play amateur psychologist here," he said carefully. "Your life is your own business. But...I just can't help but wonder if the issue we're talking about here isn't the same one that caused problems for us."

"I don't know what you're talking about." Her voice was cool, her words measured.

"I'm talking about you not letting me in. You told me once that you liked me because I didn't push you too much," he reminded her.

"I never said that!" Gillian rushed to her own defense. "Maybe I said it was *one* of the reasons, but it wasn't the only—"

"Okay, okay!" Keith raised one hand, as if to ward off her words. "I'm not accusing you of anything. I'm just telling you what I've observed."

"And what is that?"

"'*That*,' my dear, is the fact that you won't let me get close. Maybe I'm not the only one you've done this with. Maybe you aren't letting *anyone* close. It makes perfect sense: You're afraid of what might happen if you give away too much of your heart."

"I don't think that's true," Gillian protested weakly. But, even to herself, the defense fell flat.

"I'm not telling you what to believe," Keith told her. "I'm just giving you something to think about. Maybe it'll help you someday in your next relationship." Gillian's heart sank. Keith was determined. It really was the end. "Maybe with Max," he suggested.

Gillian closed her eyes. Her world was crumbling. The thought was more than she could consider. Opening them again, she reached out and squeezed his hand one last time. "I hate this, Keith. I really do. I never meant for it to be so hard."

"I know," he said softly and returned the pressure of her fingers.

"I'm sorry about everything," she said with feeling.

"Don't be," Keith told her kindly. "Everything happens for a reason. I just know it." He flashed her the last bit of smile he held in his eyes. "No regrets...okay?"

"Okay." Gillian managed a weak smile of her own as she reached for her glass of water and raised it to him. "To you," she said sentimentally, feeling a warm tenderness toward Keith for the first time—too late.

"Oh no," Keith answered, confidence in his voice. "To the future."

Two crystal goblets met with a solid *clink*.

"To the future."

Eleven

It's a vice to trust all, and equally a vice to trust none.

SENECA, *LETTERS TO LUCILIUS*

August 10, 1987

Eight days have passed since Max promised he'd be thinking about me. He said he'd be praying for me, too, but I haven't felt any different. Mom told me once that God answers prayers differently than we think he will. She says his answers are big, like he is, so they take more time than ours do. Sometimes years. She says it takes even more years for us to be able to see what he did—if we ever see it at all. I sure hope I'll be able to see it someday. Things seem pretty chaotic right now.

I went over to Jenny's this afternoon. It's the first time since the whole, ugly Matt Ross incident. I've apologized probably a dozen times, and she finally says she forgives me, but I don't think she really does. Things aren't the same anymore. I suppose we'll still be friends at school, but that's probably about it. I don't think I'll go over there again. It'll be a long summer—Jenny's the only friend who lives within biking distance. (Mom's pretty picky about how far she'll let me go.) But I'd rather be lonely than rejected.

One good thing has come out of all this, though. Without Jenny around, I've spent a lot more time by myself. I used to feel like I needed to be around someone all the time. But who have I got now?

Mom? Too busy. Dad? Yeah, right. Sometimes I don't even see him for days. Actually, I don't really mind so much being on my own. I think I'm getting used to it.

I wonder if Max really has been thinking about me? He still comes by to see my dad every week, but lately he's been coming early every time. I always get a chance to talk to him then. He tells me about what he's learning in school, how much he loves the stars. I'm actually starting to love them again, too, because of him.

He asks me stuff, too, like what do I want to study in college? I told him I wanted to be an oceanographer. I don't really, but it sounded better than admitting I had no idea. He seemed pretty impressed.

It's hard for me to imagine what my life is going to be like when I'm all grown-up. It feels so far away. I'm sixteen now, almost there. But when I think back to when I was twelve, it seems like a whole lifetime ago. I wonder what I'll be like in three years. In thirty? I wonder who I'll be. I hardly know who I am today. At the beginning of the summer, I wrote that I know who I am, but it's not true. I feel like I'm changing. And I'm a little afraid of what the future holds. It seems like there isn't anything I can count on to stay the same. Thank goodness for Max. I don't know what I'd do if I didn't have his visits to look forward to. Everyone needs hope, I'm sure of it.

And right now, Max is all the hope I've got.

August 7, 1997

"Hey, Gilly." Max poked his curly brown head past the door of her tiny office. He held up a large manila envelope. "Merry Christmas, kiddo," he quipped. "Ed just sent over your ticket to California."

Gillian passed one hand over her weary eyes. "Huh? Christmas? My what?"

Max stared at her. "Your airline ticket. You know... Pasadena. The observatory at Palomar. Great big telescope. You. Research. For me. Next month. Does any of this ring a bell?"

"Of course…Max, I'm sorry." She blinked against the light behind his head and tried to collect her thoughts. "I'm afraid my head is somewhere else today."

"Someplace fun, I hope."

Gillian snorted derisively. "I wish."

Max eyed her sympathetically. "Want to talk about it?"

"No, that's all right." She pushed her lopsided office chair away from the desk and rolled two feet over to her monstrous metal file cabinet. What would Max say if he knew her thoughts had recently been centered upon *him?* There was no way she was going to risk finding out. Some things she just had to keep to herself. "Life's just pretty confusing right now."

"Yeah. It gets that way sometimes," Max agreed. He stepped into the room and leaned his lanky body against the door frame. "I wouldn't worry too much, though," he said confidently. "Things will work out, Gilly. They always do." Gillian smiled. She was getting used to Max's little pep talks. She was even beginning to sort of like them. "Good things, too," he assured her. "Who knows? Maybe something to do with Keith?" If she wasn't so depressed, she might have laughed. Max had never seemed overly excited about her boyfriend, even after meeting him the night Keith had come by early to take her out to dinner. This wasn't just casual conversation—Max was fishing for something. And not too subtly, either.

It had been almost a week since she'd seen Keith, and so far she'd managed to keep the new status of their relationship a secret. After that terrible dinner, it had taken all her self-control *not* to call up Max and beg to see him that very night. At this point, even though she held him at arm's length, he was still the closest friend she had. Things had smoothed over a bit with Bridget, though they were still a bit awkward. But even during the best of times, Gillian hadn't known her roommates all that well. Right now, with her life in turmoil, she felt her lack of

151

connections more deeply than ever before.

She opened one metal file drawer with a *bang* and carefully avoided making eye contact with Max. Even though she'd wanted to tell him what had happened, the whole subject felt incredibly dangerous. What if she accidentally revealed the *full* extent of her conversation with Keith? What if Max figured out that she liked him? There was no question that the feelings were one-sided, and what could make for a more awkward working situation than that? She was going to have to tell him about breaking up with Keith *sometime,* though.

"Actually, I don't think it's too likely that God has something planned for Keith and me, since we broke up last week," she confessed.

"Really?" Max took a couple of steps farther into the room. "*Ohhhhhh.* Wait a minute. So, that's it. No wonder you've been moping around here all week!"

"Oh, stop it," she scolded him. "I have *not* been moping."

"Oh no? Well, what do you call this?" Max grabbed his lower lip between thumb and forefinger and gave every appearance of trying to pull it up over his nose. Hunching his shoulders, he dragged his arms at his side and began to circle the room. Gillian laughed in spite of herself. "There. See? That's better. That's what's been missing around here."

"What is?"

"Your laugh."

"Yeah, well…" The smile disappeared from her face. "It's been missing in a lot of places lately."

The look Max gave Gillian was one of compassion. Grabbing a stack of files from the chair opposite her, he placed them on the floor and sat down, finally managing to catch her eye. "Look, Gilly, I'm not going to push you to talk about anything you don't want to. Maybe there's more to it than you want to share. But I want you to know that if you need someone to listen—"

"Thanks, Max." Gillian managed a halfhearted smile. It wasn't his fault that she had made such a mess of things. "Really, it's not all that complicated. And not that much of a shock when I really think about it." She sighed. "It's the same problem I've had in all my relationships. I just don't want to let anyone get too close, you know?" She looked at him anxiously, hoping for a sign that he understood.

"I'm not sure I know what you mean," he said uncertainly.

Gillian closed her eyes, gathering her thoughts. What on earth had compelled her to start talking about this with him? This was the last subject she wanted to explore with Max, but there was no way out of it now. "It's just that...when I was younger, there were several people in my life who I really loved," she explained. "It just seemed like whatever I did, I ended up losing them. I wound up feeling crushed and alone. I always gave every bit of myself, and I lost every bit of myself as well." *I can predict exactly what Max will say next,* she thought. *"There's no such thing as giving away too much love...."*

"That's the thing about loving people," he said thoughtfully. "Sometimes they don't love you back very well. Or at all. People are pretty fallible creatures, Gilly. There's a lot of risk involved." He looked at her seriously. "Maybe the problem is, you're giving too much of yourself. Or maybe your expectations are a little too high."

"What do you mean, giving too much of myself? I've hardly been giving anything at all." This from the man who talked so much of God. Hadn't she heard somewhere that *God is love?*

"Maybe that's the way it is now, but it doesn't sound like that was always the case. What were you like when you were a little girl? Before I knew you? What was it like to love someone then...say your dad, for example?"

"I don't know....I just *loved* him."

"How did you feel when he wasn't there for you?"

153

Gillian squirmed in her seat. "Well...*devastated,* of course. He was everything to me when I was little."

"'Devastated' is a pretty strong word."

"Well, what do you expect?" she answered testily. "I was a little girl. Dad was *everything* to me." *Just like you were when I was a teenager.*

"I know," Max said gently. "I'm not trying to say you should have felt anything different. Your feelings are perfectly normal. I'm just trying to get to the heart of how you're responding." Gillian relaxed a tiny bit. "Children are naturally trusting," Max theorized. "But as we go through life, eventually we learn that not everyone is trustworthy. People fail each other—sometimes on purpose, sometimes without intending to. We can't open ourselves up fully to everyone we meet. It's important to hold back a bit."

"But that's what I'm doing now."

Max shook his head. "I'm not talking about shutting people out, Gilly. And I'm not suggesting that you limit the love you feel or give. I'm just saying that you need to protect yourself...to be careful about what you give away of yourself, and what you expect to get in return. If you give, expecting something you may not get, it can be pretty painful. But if you're able to give for the sake of giving and take whatever comes your way, it becomes much easier to love."

"It's hard for me to give *anything* these days," she said shakily.

"I know." Max's voice was gentle. "You're afraid of getting hurt again, aren't you?"

"Yeah," Gillian practically whispered. "I guess I am. It's hard for me to trust anyone anymore."

Max drew one hand roughly across his chin and gave her a thoughtful look. "I don't want to get too pushy here," he said sincerely, "but maybe there's someone in your past that you need to forgive...."

154

Gillian looked at him in surprise. She hadn't even entertained the thought. "Why do you say that?"

"Well, it sounds as though you're still carrying around a lot of hurt from a long time ago. Forgiveness is a powerful thing, Gilly. Maybe it's time to let those things go so you can move on."

Gillian's soft brown eyebrows furrowed together as she tried to process what he was saying. She wasn't an angry person, not the type to hold grudges...was she?

"Sometimes people do the best they can, but they still fail to meet our expectations or needs," Max said carefully. Gillian considered this, thinking back to the way she had behaved toward Bridget and—years ago—her best friend, Jenny. She had failed them, too. Neither one of them had truly forgiven her. Would it have made an impact on her life—and theirs—if they had? She thought about her family.

"Like my dad, you mean?" she asked.

"Sure, like your dad. I could tell you guys were having problems, way back when I was coming to your house to work with him." He threw her a half-smile. "You'd come downstairs and try to act like this cool, rebellious teenager. But your eyes would always drift over to your father. No matter where he went, what he did, what he said, you were watching, waiting to take it all in. It was obvious that you loved him and wanted more from him than he was willing to give."

She hadn't thought Max had noticed, but he had. Suddenly a lump rose in her throat, and she swallowed it down hard. "And you think that's why I have problems now? Because I didn't have a good relationship with my dad?" The idea of blaming someone else was both welcoming and disturbing.

"Not your dad, specifically, although I think that relationship has had a huge impact on your life. Every relationship has an impact, really. We all need love. And when we don't get

155

what we need, we cope the best we can. It sounds like the way you cope has definitely impacted your relationship with Keith. Maybe others."

"I'm not doing this on purpose!" Gillian wailed. "If I knew how to change, I would. But it's not that easy."

"Of course it's not." Max sounded surprised. "Change never is. We all fear change. Look at Copernicus or Galileo. They found evidence that the sun and not the earth was the center of the galaxy. But look at what these men went through—and how long the world fought against believing in the truth. Change is threatening. Everything within us resists it."

Gillian gave him a sidelong glance. She couldn't help feeling like a charity case. "Do you really think my expectations are too high?"

"I have no idea," Max told her honestly. "We've never talked about your expectations. I wonder, though, about what you're willing to accept in a relationship."

Gillian eyed him warily. "Meaning?"

"Some people set their standards too low. They settle for someone who hurts them—physically or emotionally or spiritually," he explained. "Others raise the bar too high. As a result, no one can measure up." Max leaned back in his chair and stared at the sterile, white-tiled ceiling, the way he often did when he was mulling over a favorite theory. "From what you've been saying, I wonder if maybe you're the second kind."

"I wish you wouldn't make me sound so…dysfunctional," she complained. "Just because I don't want to get hurt."

Max sat up again and leaned toward her. "If you're looking for relationships with people who will never hurt you, Gilly, I'd be willing to bet that you're out of luck," he said simply. "But you know, a person doesn't have to *not* hurt you, *ever*, in order to love you well. You'll have fights, you'll be inconsiderate to each other at times. That happens. That's just life."

"What if the person you love doesn't even stick around long enough to *be* inconsiderate?" Gillian thought of the long nights when there had been no one at home except her and her mother because her father had to work late. She remembered the day Max had walked out of her life. She suddenly felt a faint stinging behind her eyelids.

"Well, then you've learned something, and you won't give as much of yourself to that person the next time," he said reasonably. "But it doesn't have to have a negative impact on every other relationship that follows."

Gillian made a terrible face. "Yuck. This is no fun. Why do relationships have to be so *hard?*" she said dramatically.

Max laughed. "Oh, come on. It's not as bad as all that. You've got your whole life ahead of you, Gilly. There's plenty of reason to hope. Besides," he said grinning, "I've got just the thing to cheer you up. What are you doing Tuesday night?"

"I don't know," Gillian grumbled. "My social calendar is looking pretty open all of a sudden."

"Great!" He ignored her sullen tone. "The Perseid meteor shower will be visible this week. Tuesday's the best night. Come on. You *know* you want to go. It's the *Perseids*. Up to one hundred shooting stars per hour. Think how many wishes you could make!"

"Yeah?" That caught Gillian's attention. She sat up straight in her chair. "What time are you thinking about going?"

"Eleven at the earliest. Maybe not until midnight. The later the better. They'll be higher in the sky the longer we wait, but then you know that. Maybe we can take along a snack or something."

Gillian felt her face heating up. "I have to admit, it sounds great. The thing is…I'm just not sure."

Max eyed her curiously. "What's the matter, Gilly?"

By this time, she was certain her cheeks had to be bright

red. "I don't know if it's a good idea for us to, you know...go out together." The words came out in a rush. "I mean, Keith and I just broke up a week ago, and—"

"I agree."

Gillian stopped short. "What?"

"I said, I agree," Max told her calmly but not unkindly.

"You mean you weren't—" Her hands flew to her cheeks. "Oh, my gosh. I'm so embarrassed! Max, please...forgive me. I didn't mean to imply that—" She climbed out of her chair and retreated to the window, trying to get as far away as possible. "You must think I'm an idiot, assuming that you would want to ask me out!"

"There's nothing idiotic about that idea," Max said in a low voice. His words only added to her confusion.

"What are you saying?" Gillian watched as he rose from his chair and came to stand beside her.

"I'm saying that I'm very attracted to you, Gilly," he said in a low voice.

"You are?" Gillian's heart started doing the rumba. "Wait. Back up. You lost me. I thought you weren't. You just said you *didn't* want to ask me out."

For once, Max seemed uncertain about what to say. "Honestly, Gilly, I'm not sure what I want," he admitted. "I mean, I *do,* in a way. I think it would be great to spend more time together, get to know each other again. But after what you've said, I'm not sure you're ready for that, or that you'd even want it. And even if you did, I don't know that it would be such a good idea for us."

Gillian's head was swimming. Were they really having this conversation? It didn't seem possible. "Why not?" Her voice sounded far away and foreign to her own ears.

"We're just in very different places spiritually." Max looked as though the words pained him. "I don't *ever* want you to feel ashamed for being where you're at. Your spiritual journey is your own—I can't force the issue for you," he said, and Gillian could tell that he meant it. "But, at the same time, I know how much God means to me. I couldn't pretend it was any other way. And I'd just worry about that becoming a conflict for us."

"Like it was for my parents," she said dully.

"Yeah," Max said ruefully. "Like it was for them."

Gillian nodded slowly. "My mom once told me that she and Dad had a lot of problems, but the worst was not connecting spiritually. She said that made it even harder to find common ground in other areas." A feeling of sadness gripped her heart. The thing she had wanted for so long was almost within her grasp...yet still far out of reach. "I think that's just one more thing I'm afraid of."

"Me, too," said Max soberly.

Gillian averted her eyes, focusing on the bright green leaves of the sugar maple outside her window. "The problem is, I don't know how I could find someone who believes the same thing I do, when I'm not even sure what *I* believe." Suddenly, she felt terribly alone.

Max reached out and squeezed her hand with gentle fingers. "I think that's a pretty important thing to know...regardless of *who* you decide to share your life with."

The words rang true in Gillian's mind. He was right. She had been running for too long. She turned to him to express her gratitude, but at the sight of his warm compassionate face her heart welled up and she could not find the words. If only *he* was the one she would spend her life with....

Finally, she managed, "Max? About what you said before?"

"Yes?"

She drew in a deep breath and let it out slowly. "Do you really like me? I mean, *really?*"

Max smiled then—a smile that started at his lips and

reached all the way to his eyes. "I really do."

"Yeah, well…" At his confession, Gillian could not keep a grin from slowly spreading across her own face. "I guess I kinda like you, too. In fact, I've always had a little crush on you."

"I know," Max said playfully and began to toy with her fingers, which he still held in his hand.

"You *know?*"

"Of course! The way you followed me around when you were a kid? It was adorable. You were the sweetest thing…."

"Oh, stop. You're making me sick." She laughed and tried to pull away, but he held her hand fast.

"I'm *serious,*" Max said. "The sad part was, you were seven years younger than me. Just a baby."

"Come on, I was *not* a *baby*…." Gillian tried to protest, but she could not keep the grin from her face.

"Ah, yes you were." Max was merciless in his teasing. "But I couldn't help noticing you anyway. You had those incredible hazel eyes. And that beautiful, honey-colored hair." He reached and gently lay his free hand upon the soft golden strands at the back of her neck. "And…"

"And what?" she prompted breathlessly.

Max's expression grew serious. "And…there was just something about you that captured my heart, Gilly. Even though you were just a kid, I remember thinking how much I liked you, how I would have wanted to go out with you if I'd still been in high school, too."

She stared at him incredulously. "You're making this up."

"No," he insisted. "Really, I'm not. I'll admit, it was just a fleeting thought at the time. It never really went anywhere back then. But when I saw you again in Ed's office—" Tenderly he stroked her hair. Gillian let her eyelids fall, losing herself in the moment. And then it was gone.

Max stepped back abruptly, staring at his hand as if he'd

never seen it before. "Gilly, this is crazy! We can't be talking like this. We've already said that it wouldn't be a good idea for us to date."

Gillian froze and watched him back away, feeling his withdrawal as deeply as if she were losing a part of her self. *What were you thinking, Gillian? Didn't Max just get through explaining that you need to protect your heart? You lost him once—you're not going to get to keep him this time.* "You're right," she said, carefully keeping her voice under control. There was no point in letting him see how deeply his words hurt her.

"It wouldn't be a good idea *right now,* anyway," he said thoughtfully.

"Why do you say that?" Gillian gave him a funny look as she stepped away. "You don't really expect anything to change?"

"Don't underestimate the power of God, Gilly," Max said mysteriously. "When he's involved, anything is possible."

Twelve

As a man thinketh so is he, and as a man chooseth so is he.
EMERSON, "SPIRITUAL LAWS," ESSAYS: FIRST SERIES

August 13, 1987

Mom and Dad had another fight this morning. Mom wants me to start going to church with her. Dad tells her he doesn't want me getting messed up with all that religious garbage. I asked him about it once. He said it was up to me whether I wanted to go or not, but that he didn't want me to come crying to him when it turned out to be a big scam. He looked at me like I was an idiot for even considering it, and we haven't talked about it since. Mom hasn't been able to get me to go with her, either.

I don't know why I should have to decide, anyway. I'm only sixteen years old, after all. I've got plenty of time to decide what I think. I don't want to have to worry about it when there's all this pressure on me to pick which side is right. One of these days I'll figure it out for myself. In the meantime, I just want to be left alone.

Max thinks it's possible to believe in both science and God. But Dad hasn't liked Max very much since the day he said that. Poor Max pushed all of his buttons, and now Dad's really cranky with him. I've seen them arguing on Max's way out to the car. Sometimes I can even hear Dad yelling while Max is in the study with him. Max doesn't come over early very much anymore. He doesn't even like to *come—I can tell by the look on his face. I sure wouldn't want to be in his shoes.*

It makes me sad, though, that I don't get to see him. It's been a hard summer. Jenny hasn't been around in weeks. Mom and Dad are fighting more and more all the time. It feels like everything around me is changing.

I wish there was some kind of order to my life, but right now it seems impossible. And to tell you the truth, some days I'm afraid to find out what's going to happen next.

August 11, 1997

"I cannot *believe* I let you talk me into this!" Gillian yawned widely as she followed in Max's steps. "Are we crazy? It's almost midnight! I should have been in bed hours ago." Carefully she placed each foot on the ground, trying not to stumble as they made their way through Colonial Park's gentle darkness.

"Spoilsport," Max said fondly. In his hands he carried a massive red, plaid picnic blanket, a bag of gooey macaroons, and a bottle of sparkling water. "You must be getting old."

"I beg your pardon?" Gillian huffed. "Just because I make sure my body gets enough sleep? I don't think so. Besides, I'm only twenty-six." She eyed him critically. "And you, my friend, have no room to talk."

"I'll have you know I am a very *young* thirty-three," Max told her cheerfully, tromping on ahead.

"No kidding," Gillian muttered under her breath. "You've got the energy of a hyperactive ten-year-old." Then, more loudly, "Could we *please* slow down? I've got a rock in my shoe. Besides, I thought we were there."

"Just a little farther. Stop complaining," he laughed and led her deeper into the clearing. Gillian looked around, wondering what kind of animals might be watching them from the surrounding forest. She tilted her head back and looked up at the black walnut trees, wondering if she was at that moment being observed by owls.

A sudden burst of light caught her eye. "Wait! Look!" She stopped and pointed up to the northeast, toward the Perseid's radiant, its point of origin in the sky. "Did you see it? That was a bright one!"

"Missed it. Okay, you win. Let's stop." Max handed her the Thermos and brown paper bag, then snapped the fuzzy red blanket open with a flourish and spread it out for them to sit on.

"Mmm, this is nice." Gillian sighed happily as she sat down and leaned back on one arm. As she spoke, Max settled down beside her, just a couple feet from where her hand rested. "Very peaceful. It reminds me of the times when I was a little girl and my dad used to take me out to look at the stars."

Max raised an eyebrow. "Really? Dr. Spencer did that? That sure seems awfully sentimental of him."

"Yeah, it was. Pretty out of character, huh?" Gillian made a face. "Well, don't worry. It didn't last. As I got older, Dad started acting more like a teacher than a father. I resisted, and he stopped taking me out after that."

Max looked horrified. "That must have felt *terrible*," he said sympathetically.

Gillian shrugged. She hardly thought about it any more. "It wasn't that bad."

"Maybe not anymore, but it must have been horrible at the time." He lay back against the soft cotton cover and folded both arms under his head.

Gillian frowned. It had been a long time since she'd thought about the situation, but...actually, Max was right. It *had* been horrible. It was so disappointing, in fact, that she had cried for a week after her dad refused to take her stargazing for the first time. He said he wouldn't take her back out if she refused to study the charts he had given her. That was when she first remembered feeling so terribly alone.

She turned to the man who lay beside her in the moonlight. Unaware that he was being watched, Max continued to stare at the sky above him, giving her the chance to examine him safely from behind the camouflage of night.

In the soft lighting, Gillian could barely make out Max's dark curls and the glint of his deep azure eyes. His rich brown corduroy, button-up shirt almost disappeared into the blackness. Only the white of his crewneck T-shirt gave her eyes an easy target to focus on.

She smiled at the shadowed figure. Everything about Max exuded a sense of peace and confidence. His presence was comfortable, reassuring. And he knew her so *well,* even though she had barely let him in. He cared about how she felt, and he wanted to know more about her. And, heaven help her— Gillian's heart started beating faster at the thought—she wanted to know his deepest thoughts and feelings, too.

Despite every protest she had uttered since the beginning of summer, Gillian had finally realized the truth: More than anything, she wanted to be with this man, to throw herself into his arms, to finally find out what it meant to love someone. *But...that wouldn't be right.* Gillian tried to push the thought away. Max's choice was clear. He had found a source of strength, of peace, in his God—a decision that she both respected and envied. If she had such peace, she would never do anything to jeopardize it. She couldn't expect anything less of Max.

I've got to stop thinking about this. Gillian tore her eyes from his face and scanned the sky for streaks of light. *Things aren't going to happen between Max and me,* she thought. But a second voice whispered, *Then, why are you here?* She shook her head, as if shooing away a pesky fly.

"Did your dad ever take you out to see a meteor shower?"

Max plucked a piece of meadow grass and stuck it between his teeth, the perfect picture of a preppie hillbilly.

"Sure, he did," Gillian told him. "A couple of times my mom even came along." Following Max's lead, she turned and laid her back flat against the blanket so she could see the stars better. "I remember once, she had been reading *Peter Pan* to me, and I thought the lights were fairies, flying in from Never Never Land!" As if on cue, a tiny flicker of white shot across the heavens, then disappeared. "Mom said she thought maybe the lights were angels."

Max opened his eyes wide. "*Your* mother thought that stars were angels?"

"I know, I know," Gillian laughed. "This was before she went back to church and brushed up on her facts," she explained. "But she always seemed drawn to spiritual things."

"For a minute there, I was a little bit worried about what kind of propaganda she might have been feeding you."

Gillian ignored the playful dig. "I remember one time, in particular, when Dad took me out," she said. "He must have decided that I was old enough to know the truth, because he explained all about meteors that night: the way fragments dislodge from a comet every time it passes close to the sun, and the fact that eventually these fragments separate completely from the comet, forming their own orbit around the sun."

"Whew!" Max let out a low whistle. "That's a lot of orbits."

"Tell me about it," Gillian said dryly. "It was very confusing to me as a kid. I wasn't even sure what an orbit *was*. Then, of course, he explained what caused meteor showers. I got scared and imagined our house being hit by flying boulders. He—oh, look! That was a good one!" She pointed toward a bright train of light directly overhead.

"So have you had nightmares about meteors ever since?" Max asked when it was gone.

"No, but I did for a while," she admitted. "One day I was looking in one of Dad's books, and I saw a picture of the meteor crater in Arizona. It was something like four thousand feet across, I think, and it looked like the surface of the moon to me. I just about came unglued." She chuckled at the memory. "But then Dad told me that most meteors, like the Perseid meteor shower, are just cometary debris. He said that the bigger, single pieces that fall to earth come from asteroid collisions, and that the odds of getting hit by one of those are too minuscule to even consider."

"Well, that's comforting," Max chuckled. "I *guess*."

But Gillian wasn't laughing. "I really enjoyed those meteor showers," she said softly. "There was something very...mysterious about them, the way they just appeared out of nowhere. But then my dad explained that they were regular and predictable. That was pretty disappointing to me. I had always been so excited and proud that my daddy could guess when the falling stars were coming. It made him seem sort of godlike to me."

"I can imagine." Max had turned to watch her more closely and now rested his head on one elbow.

By this time, Gillian was so lost in her memories, she barely noticed him. "I always liked the Perseids the best," she said. "And not just because it's the biggest one. Dad told me it was named after Perseus because all the meteors in that shower appear to come from that constellation. I always liked Perseus," she said. "'The Hero.' I liked the legend."

Max's eyes twinkled as he watched her face light up. "You really are a romantic at heart, aren't you?" His voice was soft and low.

"Well...maybe a little," she admitted reluctantly, dropping her hand back to her side. "When I was a child, I dreamed that a hero, just like Perseus, would come and save me from some horrible fate."

"What kind of horrible fate?"

Gillian pursed her lips together, considering. "I don't remember, really. Monsters. Dragons, I suppose. That sort of thing." Suddenly, she realized he was staring at her. "Silly stuff." She cleared her throat nervously.

"When did you stop being a romantic?" Max asked gently.

If anyone else had asked the question, she would have been offended. But coming from Max, it sounded like an inquiry and not an accusation. "I'm not sure," Gillian answered slowly. "Life just didn't work out the way I thought it would." She thought for a moment, searching the recesses of her mind for some explanation that would make sense to him...and to her. "I don't know what happened, really. I guess I finally just decided that I didn't need a hero, that I could take care of myself." The words were partially true. She liked being an independent woman. But somehow, her life had ended up being a lot lonelier than she had planned.

"And you're okay with that?"

"I don't know," she admitted sadly. "Sometimes it's fine. I actually like not having to depend on a man to take care of me. I like feeling strong." Her eyes followed a thin trail of white that flashed past Perseus's bright alpha star. "The problem is, I don't *always* feel strong."

Max continued to watch her carefully. "You know, even if you found your hero in this lifetime, he probably wouldn't be there for you *always,* anyway."

"Yeah..." Gillian sat up stiffly and wrapped her arms around her knees. The hot summer night was finally beginning to cool. Her sleeveless denim shirt left her vulnerable to the night air, and she could feel the goose bumps rising up on her skin. "It would be nice if there was someone I could count on, no matter what."

Max nodded but said nothing. The two sat together, silently, for several long minutes. "You know what I thought falling stars were, when I was a kid?" he asked finally. "I thought they were signs from God. Reminders that he's there."

"What...like little flares?"

"No." Max grinned. "I thought it was a symbol. Like the rainbow. My mother told me that God sent rainbows to remind us that he promised never to flood the earth again. I thought maybe he sent the stars to remind us that he's out there."

"Huh." Gillian thought about this. "Well, they certainly do get people's attention."

"Do you know what the Native Americans believed about meteors?" Max asked.

"Hunh-unh." Gillian gave a little shrug. "I suppose they thought it was some kind of sign?"

"A lot of them did. The Blackfoot thought it was a warning that illness would come to their tribe. And the Shawnee thought the meteors were beings running away from some terrible danger."

"How sad!" She looked up as a shimmering light fell to the horizon. "To think that anything so beautiful could mean something so terrible."

"The strangest belief of all was that of the Nunamiut Eskimos and some tribes in southern California and Louisiana. They believed that meteors were...well, the, uh..." Max sounded almost embarrassed. Gillian turned to look at him, but she couldn't see his face clearly in the darkness.

"What did they think they were?"

"Let's just call it, uh, star 'waste.'"

"What do you mean, 'waste'? Do you—oh! I get it!" Gillian stifled a giggle. "All right, *now* you're definitely pulling my leg." She started punching him on the arm with one small fist.

"No, really!" Max cowered, taking the beating. "I'm not making this up! I studied it in—ow!" He laughed and rolled away, out of her reach, then lay down on his stomach, facing her. "And then there's the Pawnee legend about a man named Pahokatawa." His voice dropped to a whisper, as if he were sharing a terrible ghost story.

"Forget it." Gillian waved one open palm at him, as if signaling for him to stop. "I don't believe you anymore." She folded her arms across her chest and turned away, her chin in the air.

Max was undaunted. "The Pawnees believed that after being killed by an enemy," he continued on in an eerie, singsong voice, "Pahokatawa was eaten by animals, then brought back to life by the gods. He returned in the form of a meteor and told his people that when a shower of stars fell toward earth, they did not have to be afraid because it was *not* a sign that the world was coming to an end."

She turned her head and looked back at him, interested in spite of herself.

"Years later, when the massive Leonid meteor storm fell in 1833," Max went on, "the people started to panic. But the tribal leader reminded them of what Pahokatawa had said, and they all were comforted."

Gillian planted her elbows against her knees and rested her chin in her hands. "It seems like people who look to the sky usually find something that makes them think about gods or one God," she said thoughtfully.

"It's pretty much unavoidable," Max agreed. "It would be hard to come face-to-face with the universe and not consider the nature of it. I can't imagine looking at the stars and not wondering what lies beyond them." He eyed her curiously. "Do you ever wonder about it, Gilly?"

"Yeah," she admitted quietly. "I guess I do. Probably more these days than ever before." In fact, since Max had returned and started talking about God, she'd thought about it nearly every day. It was hard not to feel like something was missing from her life after being around someone like Max, whose world seemed so complete.

"Why more now?" Max asked evenly. He gave her a look of genuine interest and concern. "What's different these days?"

"Well, you for one thing," Gillian said honestly, the words spilling out before she could stop them. Her willingness to open up surprised her. She had consumed no alcohol, but somehow she felt tipsy-drunk, perhaps on open skies and childhood memories. It had been a long time since she had felt safe enough to share her deepest feelings. There was just something about Max that made her believe he cared and would understand. "It's been a while—maybe eight years—since I've been around someone who talked about God every day. It's almost as if he's your friend," she observed. The words came out flat and matter-of-fact, almost clinical.

"He is my friend, Gilly," Max said warmly.

Gillian shook her head in astonishment. "I can't imagine what that must be like." She looked at him with interest, unable to conceal her curiosity any longer. "How does it feel? I mean, it's not like you can call him on the phone and talk to him, or go to the movies together, right? It seems like it would be hard to believe he's even there."

"Well, I don't call him on the phone," Max laughed. "But I do talk to him every day."

Gillian nodded at the obvious reference to prayer. "But he can't talk back."

"Sure he can. He does," Max said confidently.

Gillian turned and eyed him with suspicion. "Max. Please tell me you don't hear voices."

He smiled at her, his eyes dancing. "Not exactly. It's more like I feel him speaking to my heart. Sometimes it comes as a flash of insight. Sometimes a Bible verse comes to mind—one I've memorized or read recently. At other times it's just a feeling, a sense of his love, or his compassion, washing over me."

"But don't you ever feel funny, talking to someone you can't see?" she pushed. "Does it ever feel like he's—I don't know—your invisible friend or something? Like…what if you're being fooled?"

"Are you asking if I ever doubt God's existence?"

A sudden feeling of trepidation grabbed Gillian's heart. Was her suggestion sacrilegious? Would God punish her for asking such a thing? As the thought crossed her mind she realized, to her own amazement, that her belief in God was intact. It was, in fact, very strong, if her feelings of fear were any indication. Surely she couldn't be afraid of someone she didn't think was even there? She looked up to find Max staring at her, waiting for her response.

"Um, yeah," she said nervously.

"Well." Max thought for a moment. "Actually, there are times when I read some other physicist's interpretation of scientific facts, and I wonder if maybe my own beliefs are incorrect." As he spoke, he continued to stare up at the night sky. "During those times, I sometimes think that I might be fooling myself. But then my heart kicks in, and I relive all the tangible experiences I've had—all the times I've felt and seen God working in my life—and I focus in on what I know to be true." He propped himself up on one elbow and turned to face her.

"Then there are other times when I face troubles in life—when I'm hurt or alone, when I can't understand what God is doing, and I feel abandoned or betrayed by him." Gillian couldn't believe her ears. Max? Doubting God? It didn't seem likely. Yet here he was, confessing it with his own mouth. "Sometimes my heart feels empty," Max went on, "and it questions whether he really loves me, whether he really exists. But I know that I've made a conscious choice to follow him. My mind reminds me that I've made a rational decision, based on what I know to be true, to put my faith in him." His eyes searched hers earnestly. "Sure, I have doubts, Gilly. I suppose most people do, from time to time. But I believe that God in his grace understands our doubts. That he sees us through those times and gives us reminders that he is here. Sometimes we read those reminders with our minds and sometimes with our hearts."

"Reminders like the stars," Gilly whispered.

"Mm-hm." Max smiled. "Like little flares."

She grinned sheepishly.

"What about you, Gilly?" Max asked gently. "You told me that you're not sure what you believe. That must be hard, with your mom being a Christian and all. I'm sure she talked about God a lot. That uncertainty must be a source of real inner conflict for you."

Gillian stared at him, her eyes wide. He did understand. Better than she did, perhaps. It seemed he had intuitively sensed the truth she'd been trying to deny for years—but could not longer avoid. "Yeah, there is." She pushed back the impulse to reach out one hand and give his arm a tiny squeeze. "Mom told me about God lots of times. She said that he loved me so much, he sent his son to die for my sins."

"And where did that leave you?"

"More confused than ever, I think." She began to fiddle absently with the lace of her white sneakers. "You know, Max, it's not that I don't believe in God, or Jesus." Her tone raised in pitch as her anxiety level increased. "It's just that I got so tired of being in the middle of the Big Debate, you know? Mom said one thing, Dad another. I didn't want to have to choose, so I guess I put off thinking about it. And now...now I'm afraid to." Gillian's hands fell helplessly to her sides. She couldn't believe what was coming out of her mouth. She'd never talked with anyone about this before, but the words were all horribly true.

"What are you afraid of?"

Gillian looked at Max. His expression was gentle, accepting... just like his heart. "Lots of things, I guess. For one, I'm afraid of believing, then finding out that it was just a pipe dream." She crossed her legs and leaned toward him, speaking in earnest. "Okay, let's say I go ahead and do what you say...I read my Bible. I pray. I accept that Jesus paid the price for my sins. What then, Max?" she asked. The scientist in her had taken over, but her voice sounded desperate. "What if I give my heart to him, and then it turns out he doesn't exist? What if in the end it isn't true?" She looked up at the stars, anxiously, as if she might find her answer there. "I'm afraid of choosing wrong," she said helplessly.

"Do you think that maybe there's some other god?" There was no hint of judgment in his tone, only concern.

"No, that's not it."

"Then, why do you have to be afraid of choosing wrong?"

"I'm just...afraid of being disappointed, Max." Gillian searched for the right words. How could she explain to him the logic that barely made sense in her own heart? "I don't dare hope, if there's a chance it might not be true. My dad was right when he said there's no absolute proof that there's a God. You said so yourself. If only it was provable, then maybe I could risk it. But the way it is...I just don't know if I can."

Max thought for a moment. "Remember ten years ago, when I told you I wanted to prove there was a God?" he finally said. Gillian nodded wordlessly. "Well, I never did." He sounded accepting, not bitter. "Sometimes, especially when scientists make new discoveries that support what I believe, I think that one day it will happen: we'll find definitive proof of God's existence, and then everyone will have to agree.

"But at other times—and this is most of the time—I figure the mystery is all a part of God's plan."

"But why wouldn't God just want us to know?" she asked helplessly. "Why do we have to guess?"

"It's not guessing, Gilly," Max said easily. "It's faith. There's a difference. You don't have to hold your brain in check to believe in him. There's plenty of evidence out there that supports his existence. Science and religion don't have to compete. In fact, I believe science adds to our understanding of faith and vice versa. Unfortunately, I can't offer you the absolute proof you want. All I can tell you is that everything I've learned in my studies, everything I've seen, points to him. And everything I've experienced in life has shown me that there's a void in my life that only he can fill." At the edge of the clearing, a night owl cried out from the shelter of an ancient white oak.

"You can't prove the unprovable, Gillian," Max said simply. "And for now, that's the way it is. That's the way God made it. But just because something isn't obvious doesn't mean it isn't real. Faith is a choice. Just as the men and women of the Renaissance chose to believe either that the sun revolves around the earth or that the earth revolves around the sun, you have a choice to make about God."

Gillian sat quietly, considering this. Was it really so hard to believe what Max was saying? To do what he was suggesting? After all those years of waffling, had the time come to make a decision for or against Christ? She'd always said that she would figure out what she believed about God one day. Would a better time ever come? All the evidence was in. She'd been studying the origins of the universe for years and still had no reason to believe God didn't exist. In fact, much of the evidence did—as Max suggested—support a creationist perspective. And if God was the Creator...then wasn't he also the father of Jesus, as the Bible stated? The truth was, she'd thought about God before, but she'd never tried to know him. Never made a choice to follow Jesus. But if what Max said was true, she had nothing to lose…and everything to gain. What if she just let go of her desire to know, to remain safe and in control? Perhaps it was finally time to take that leap of faith. And yet, still something held her back.

"Gilly," Max said seriously, "is the idea of walking with God at all appealing to you?"

"More than I'd like to admit," she answered softly. As she spoke, her eyes filled with tears she didn't even bother trying to hide. What would be the point? She was alone, desperate. Max knew it. He'd been watching her for weeks, and he knew she was hurting. "I know I sound pretty detached sometimes," she said sadly. "But the truth is, I'm sort of envious when you talk about your relationship with God. You say that Jesus is a friend to you. I can't even imagine such a thing. I'd give anything to have someone like that. Someone who wouldn't leave me, who accepted me just as I am…" Her voice trailed off as she became lost in her own thoughts.

Max reached out one cool hand and touched the warmth of her cheek. "God is like that, Gilly."

Gillian felt a tear fall from her eye and roll onto his fingers. "I want to believe it, Max," she murmured. "I really do."

"But?"

"But…Max, what if God doesn't even want me?" Her voice broke as she spoke.

Max's own eyes welled up with tears of compassion. "Oh, Gilly! What do you mean?" He cupped her cheek with his hand.

"I mean, look at me!" she exclaimed. "I'm twenty-six years old, and I've been running from him for almost that long. You love God, Max. I fear him. Do you know that? Sometimes, when I think about him, I become really afraid," she admitted tremulously. "I'm scared of dying. I'm afraid of what will happen to me." Her voice was barely recognizable, it was shaking so badly. "But I'm even more afraid of being alone. For the rest of my life. Forever…"

Max nodded somberly. "That's what hell will be like. Separation from God. The worst kind of loneliness there is."

At this, Gillian's body shook as she gave in to a whole new burst of tears. At any other time, she might have felt self-conscious. But the release of her long pent-up emotions was all consuming. There was no room for embarrassment; she felt only anguish.

"But, Gilly," Max said, his voice full of conviction, "it doesn't have to be this way." He took her by the shoulders and turned her to face him, forcing her to meet his eyes. "God does love you, Gilly. He wants to be a part of your life—now and forever. He wants to be a friend to you, too."

"But I don't deserve it, Max!" Gilly wailed.

"Of course you don't, honey," he said tenderly. "None of us do. But God forgives you."

"But he can't, Max. I'm…I'm…" She struggled to find the words. Gently, Max wiped away the tears that streamed from her eyes. "You're what, Gilly?"

"I'm…unforgivable," she said with passion. Her eyes darted about, as if searching for some way of escape.

Max looked mildly surprised but not shocked. "Why would you say that?"

Gillian shook her head helplessly. "I don't know. I just am!" She didn't understand the conviction, herself. She just knew it felt overwhelmingly true.

He put one arm around her and held her firmly as she struggled to maintain her composure. From the bag of macaroons, he pulled out two napkins which she used to wipe her eyes and nose.

"Now, let's talk about this," he said, after she had taken several deep breaths and dried her face. "Why do you feel unforgivable? Is it because you've done something you think is too terrible to forgive?"

"Well…I suppose." Gillian did feel unforgivably evil. Wasn't that why no one stayed in her life? She wasn't worth sticking around for. "Oh." Max loosened his hold on her shoulders and sat back. Suddenly, he was the one who looked uncomfortable. "Um…did you want to say what it is? I mean, I don't know if telling me—a man, I mean—is the best thing, but if you want to talk to somebody, I guess we could…"

Gillian stared at him. From the blush on his cheeks, it was clear that he suspected that it might be a sexual sin. She might as well set him straight on that, right away.

"No, Max. It's not what you're thinking. I've never gotten involved enough with any man to sleep with him."

Max looked both flustered and relieved. "Well, I didn't mean to imply that. I wasn't trying to say that you—"

She shook her head hard. "Don't give me so much credit. It's not a reflection on my virtue. There are reasons why I haven't gotten too close to any man, not the least of which was the fact that I couldn't be trusted."

Fresh tears began to fall. Tenderly, Max brushed them away. "I don't understand," he said quietly. His eyes urged her to go on.

Gillian sighed. "Max, I'm just a terrible person, that's all," she said heavily. "I hurt people. I disappointed my mom. Even my dad doesn't like me. And I'm a horrible friend." Before she had made a conscious decision to do so, Gillian found herself telling him all about Matt Ross and Jenny DeWhitt.

Silently and without interrupting, Max listened to the entire story. "Oh, Gilly." When she had finished, he put an arm around her shoulders and held her once again. "You're not horrible. You're just human. I'm sure your dad liked you, even if he was terrible at showing it. I know that I like you. And besides, even if we didn't, God likes you. Loves you, in fact."

"But I'm so…so, unworthy, Max," she protested.

Max smiled as he brushed damp tendrils of hair away from her eyes. "Unworthy people are his favorite kind, Gilly."

"What do you mean?" Despite herself, Gillian found herself looking at him hopefully, through watery eyes.

"Jesus didn't die for good people," Max explained patiently. "It says so in the Bible, over and over again. He died for the rest of us—which is all of us, incidentally—the imperfect, the flawed, the selfish, the rotten. Jenny didn't forgive you, Gillian…but she's not God. And your dad didn't love you well. But he's not God, either. Don't judge God by human standards. He's not like any person you know."

"Well…he sounds a lot like one person I know," she said with feeling. "You."

Max gave her a weak smile. "That's just because God's working in my life. It makes me happy to think he used me to demonstrate something of his love for you, Gilly—even a little bit. The truth is, though, I'm just like you. Imperfect, but loved by God."

"You really think I'm loved by God?" Gillian said tremulously.

"Yes," Max assured her. "I know you are."

Gillian pulled herself out of his embrace, sat up straight, and wiped her eyes. "Well, then I want to love him, too," she announced. Suddenly, the answer was clear to her, and she spoke with conviction. "I want to follow this Jesus of yours." She smiled timidly, relief washing over her the moment she spoke the words.

"'We love him because he first loved us,'" Max said solemnly.

"What?"

"That's what the Bible says. 'We love him because he first loved us.'"

The words sank into Gillian's heart as she wiped at her teary eyes. "The funny thing is, I'm still afraid," she confessed. "But I want to have a relationship with God, like you do," she said wistfully. "I want him to love me the way he loves you...and I want to learn what it's like to love him, too."

"Oh, Gilly." Max cupped Gillian's chin in his hand and smiled into her eyes. "God already loves you far more than you know."

She smiled back at him then, and for the first time in a long time it felt like a smile that truly reflected her soul. "I'm finally starting to believe it...just a little bit."

"Do you want me to pray with you now?" Max offered. Gillian nodded, and he reached out and took her hands in his.

"But I don't know what to say," she said nervously.

"Just tell him what you told me—what you've decided, how you feel toward him."

"Um, okay." Gillian lowered her head, then changed her mind and stared into the darkness overhead as she had so many times before. But this time, she was looking not at the stars, but past them...to what lay beyond.

"Hello, God," she said, timidly at first. "Um, Jesus...I don't know exactly what to say. I feel kind of embarrassed, in fact." She cleared her throat nervously. "But my friend Max has been telling me all about you. My mom did, too. For years she did. Remember that? She said that you died for me. I struggled with that when I was little. I felt guilty about it...but Mom said that you did it because you love me, and I just want to say I'm awful grateful. I don't think I can ever do anything to deserve it. But I want to love you and to be loved by you. And I want you to be a part of my life—like you are in Max's. Thanks, God. Ummm..." She looked at Max, her eyes pleading with him for guidance.

"Amen," he whispered.

"Yeah. Amen," she echoed. Suddenly, it was as if a heavy

load had been lifted from her back, and she almost felt like bursting into song. Beside her, Max beamed.

"All right then. A toast!" He reached for the sparkling water and plastic cups. "This is a night to celebrate." Overhead, a ball of white fire streaked across the night sky. "Kinda like fireworks, huh?" Max grinned. "Almost like the Fourth of July."

"Except this is better."

"Yeah," Max agreed. "We're not just commemorating the past. We're celebrating your future."

Gillian raised her eyes to the heavens, which now were almost completely black. Since she and Max had arrived at the park, the Perseids' radiant had risen higher in the sky, allowing for greater visibility of the fiery rain. The stream of shooting stars was constant now.

"Is it my imagination," she wondered aloud, "or are the stars actually getting brighter?"

"Gillian," Max said, his voice thick with emotion, "after what you decided tonight, I'd say everything is getting brighter."

Thirteen

Fare thee well! and if for ever,
Still for ever, fare thee well.
LORD BYRON, FARE THEE WELL

August 23, 1987

When I was a little kid, I used to get scared by lots of little things. I hated bees. And fire drills. The drills upset me even when I knew they were coming. In kindergarten, Mrs. Sherman would tell us in the morning that we were scheduled to have a drill sometime that day. I wouldn't be able to concentrate until it was over. I'd chew my thumbnail, stare out the window, and wait.... You'd think I would have been ready for it, but whenever the bell rang, my heart would leap inside my chest. My hands would sweat. Adrenaline rushed through my veins. Even though I knew it wasn't a real emergency, I was terrified of going through the whole fire-drill experience. Of course, eleven years later, I'm not frightened anymore. Just like everybody else, I learned I could live through it.

It was the same with bees. I'd be outside, minding my own business, when I'd hear it like a little plane in my ear. I'd jump up and run—in any direction—trying to get as far away as I could...as fast as I could. Getting stung by a bee was the worst thing I could imagine. Until it really happened. One day I finally got zapped by a yellow jacket...twice. It hurt like all get out, but Mom put some baking soda on it, and after that I was fine. Bees haven't scared me since.

But this...this was a different situation altogether. Exactly the opposite, in fact. I'd heard of people getting their hearts broken, but I thought it was just an exaggeration. Obviously people live through all kinds of pain. I didn't exactly look forward to getting my own heart shattered, but I never doubted that I would survive.

That was before I lost Max.

The funny thing is, it never even occurred to me that he might go away. He's a grad student at Princeton, for goodness' sake. Where's he gonna go? Other possibilities occurred to me. I imagined Angela might drug his drink and get him to propose or something. I knew he'd graduate eventually. But that was a long way off. He's got two years of school left to go. Who would have thought he'd transfer?

As it turns out, his dad has some sort of connections at Harvard and had wanted Max to go there for a long time. I guess Max liked it here because he held out for a while. Things changed, though, this summer. He said God closed one door and opened another. Dad laughed when he repeated that comment to Mom and me.

I think the truth is, my dad scared him away. It's not like Max could avoid him. Dad's his academic advisor, his "mentor," Mom says. Whatever you call it, he had the power to make Max's life miserable, and I think he did. I heard them arguing a lot over the last couple of weeks. "Debating," Dad called it. At first I was just sad. Now I feel totally destroyed.

I feel angry, too, though I'm not sure at whom. My first reaction is to want to yell at Dad. I want to run into his office and scream, "It's bad enough the way you treat me, but did you have to go and ruin things with Max, too?" I'm not sure what's stopping me. Maybe it's just knowing that it wouldn't make any difference if I did it.

A lot of my anger is with me. I mean, really, how dumb can I be? Pinning all my dreams on a guy seven years older than me. Of course he's leaving, what else would he do? He's got a life, and it has nothing to do with me. Besides, I know better than to love someone too much. It always hurts when you lose them. I learned that with

Jenny, with Dad. Even things with Mom feel bad. The more she works, the less time for me. Not that I'm trying very hard, myself. It's easier being alone. I'm starting to like it that way.

It doesn't make a lot of sense, but I feel pretty mad at Max, too. He came over here last week, for the last time. He'd already made arrangements for the transfer. He and Dad didn't have to meet again, but he wanted to bring back some books he'd borrowed. He showed up with two of them under one arm and a long cardboard box under the other.

I was sitting on the front porch when he got out of the Bug. Normally, I can't help but grin when I see him. No poker face here. But this time, it took all my willpower not to collapse into a pile of tears.

"Hi, Gilly," Max said. He put the books and box on the porch steps and sat down next to me on the swing.

"Hey." I tried not to look at him.

Max kept his eyes straight ahead, staring at the stand of white oaks across the street, just like I was.

"I guess you've heard, huh?" He kicked his legs forward, making the swing move a little.

"I guess." I bit my lip. This time I wasn't going to let him see me cry.

"Yeah, well." And that was all he said for a while.

"Harvard's a good school, you know." I don't know why he felt he had to say that.

"Sure." Max kicked his legs again and got the swing moving. The silence was awkward, but it was even more noticeable to hear nothing but the springs go squeak.

It was terrible. Awkward. Gross. I didn't know what to say, so I kept my mouth shut for once. I thought maybe Max would tell me again that he thought of me as a friend and that he was going to miss me. Part of me wanted him to say that we'd see each other again someday. "Harvard's not that far," he'd tell me. "It's a small world.

185

We're sure to bump into each other again." But he didn't say any of those things. He just kept pumping his legs, making that swing squeak.

"Is your dad around?" he finally asked me. I knew then that he was going to go. I shook my head; I couldn't make myself say the word. Max had called earlier—Mom gave Dad the message that he was coming, but he didn't bother to come back from the university. I guess maybe he's mad at Max, too.

"Well..." Max nodded toward the books. "Could you make sure he gets those?" I nodded. "And there's one other thing...." He reached down, picked up the box, and handed it to me.

I figured it had to be something else belonging to my dad, so I just took it from him and held it.

"Look inside," he told me. So I did. Inside I found a cheap-looking refracting telescope. Nothing bad, really. Just nothing like the ones my dad has. I've got a pretty nice one, myself, that sits in the back of my closet. Dad bought it for me when I was way too little to use it. A lot of things have changed since then.

"I was cleaning out my dorm room, and I came across this," Max said awkwardly. "I was thinking about that time we talked with your folks about God and the stars and the beginning of the universe, and I just wondered if maybe you might..." He shrugged his shoulders, real casual-like. "I don't really need it anymore. I've got a newer, better one. So if you want it...it's yours."

I'm not even sure what I said to him after that. I didn't especially want or need a telescope. But it was something that had belonged to him, so of course I took it. I guess I thanked him. He said something about me being a good kid, and then he got up and crawled back into the Bug one last time and drove away. I sat and stared at the end of the driveway for a long time after that. Maybe ten minutes, maybe an hour, maybe two. I'm not sure. I can still see it turning the corner, though.

I really liked that red fender.

Gillian breathed a sigh of satisfaction as the gum-chewing blond waitress presented her with her order: crisp, leafy greens, juicy strips of perfectly bronzed chicken, and bright cherry tomatoes piled high on a blue china plate. "Mmmm," she mumbled happily and stabbed at an appetizing chunk of spinach and romaine.

In the days and weeks following her decision to become a Christian, Gillian's life had been transformed. The depression that was a part of her everyday life had faded. Each morning she woke up with a feeling of hope and a sense of purpose.

Perhaps most dramatic of all was the change in Gillian's attitude toward her parents. As Max had suggested soon after they began working together, there were a number of people Gillian needed to forgive—including her mom and dad.

Never before had this seemed even remotely possible—at least where her father was concerned. Though Gillian had a number of emotional issues that involved her mother, the two women remained on reasonably favorable—if not exactly intimate—terms. Gillian rarely spoke to her dad, however, and tried to keep the few conversations they had as brief as possible. Yet shortly after her conversion, she had actually initiated two different phone calls with him and had managed to be civil—even friendly—during each one.

The healing did not take place instantly. Her emotions had not changed overnight. The truth was, Gillian still felt wounded by the ways in which her parents had loved her—and failed her. Yet though the pain remained, much of the anger had subsided. Forgiveness, Gillian was learning, was not a one-time event. It was a process—one that was difficult, but that God was walking her through.

Like Max, she was beginning to see God working in her life.

At first, his presence was not overwhelming to her. It took a while for her to even notice it. But before long, she realized that she didn't feel quite as alone. When she found herself struggling with a problem or with painful emotions, she was inexplicably compelled to offer up a brief prayer. With practice, those prayers were becoming more involved. Not overwhelmingly so, although it was sometimes a bit disconcerting to see how extensively her life was being affected. Still her relationship with God was growing, bit by bit.

As was her relationship with Max.

There again, the changes had been subtle. A cup of coffee here, a stroll after work there.... Soon she and Max were spending time together outside the office on the average of three times a week. Neither one of them referred to it as "dating," which was still a difficult thought for Gillian to entertain, and one that was more than a little threatening. If losing Max had hurt once before, how would it feel now...once she had *really* come to know him?

Despite their avoidance of the "D" word, however, it had become apparent that the bond they shared was based, not just on physics, but on their own, very real, personal chemistry. As always, Gillian felt a delighted little thrill whenever Max buzzed her on the phone to ask about some recent scientific finding, or sought her out in a physics department crowd, or smiled in a way that made her feel she had just experienced the first sunshine of the day.

Other things had changed, too. Like the way Max allowed his fingers to brush ever so slightly against hers as they were working side-by-side. Or the way he began to drape one arm casually around her shoulders whenever they went out walking together. He seemed to be constantly finding new and creative excuses for them to spend time together. Sometimes he talked Gillian into going with him to one of the many campus films or evening lectures. A couple of times, he had whisked her away to dinner in an attempt to foil what he called her "blatant workaholic tendencies." Tendencies notwithstanding, Gillian hadn't for one second resisted the rescues.

Eventually, Max had worked his way around to asking her out to a movie or two and even a concert. Not once did they discuss where their relationship was headed. Gillian tried not to think about it; it took all of her willpower just to relax and enjoy the ride.

The previous week, Max had told Gillian that they simply had been in the office for too long without a break, and that a long, relaxing walk would do them both good.

His choice of destination had been one of Gillian's favorite places: the beautiful, winding towpath along the Delaware-Raritan Canal. Over a century before, draft animals had beaten out the trail while pulling freight-laden barges along the slow, smooth canal that connected the Delaware and Raritan Rivers. Today, the trail attracted countless walkers, bicyclists, fishermen, boaters, canoeists, and horseback riders. Ever since she was a child, Gillian had loved the D & R State Park and had often tried to lose herself along the fifty-plus miles of paths that cut through the peaceful New Jersey countryside.

As she and Max walked alongside the gentle waters, Gillian was overcome by an unfamiliar sense of peace. The feeling was strange to her, as was the growing trust she felt for Max. Trusting did not come easily. Every day she woke up fearing that Max would not like her anymore, that something would cause him to withdraw, disappear. It was hard to let that fear go. But every day, Max would assure her in his own way that he was there to stay.

It was contentment, however, and not fear that she felt that day beside the narrow canal. It was fairly late, and a faint breeze rustled the nearby trees. Though the golden sun was low in the sky, Gillian felt warm clear through. In the gently flowing waters, a silver fish jumped, as if he, too, wanted to get a glimpse of love unfolding.

"Are you excited about going to California?" Max had asked, his words breaking the comfortable silence. For weeks, Gillian had been preparing for the trip to Palomar Mountain. She was excited about it and more than a little nervous. She would have liked it better if Max was going with her. But the university hadn't deemed it necessary—or cost-effective—to send them both. Gillian was the assistant. Collecting and processing the data was her job; analyzing it was Max's. She would have to go alone.

"Mm—" she said noncommittally.

Max laughed and wrapped his hand comfortably around hers. "What does 'Mm—' mean?"

Gillian had turned and given him a wide-eyed stare. "Silly boy, it's the sound someone makes when he or she feels a sense of pleasure," she teased. "As in, 'Mm—, this soup is good,' or 'Mm—, your hand is warm....'"

"Or, 'Mm—, this is a beautiful woman'?"

Gillian stopped and stared at him again, but this time her shock was real.

"Wh-what did you say?"

Max smiled, a slow, easy smile that touched his eyes and exposed his heart.

"I said, I am looking at the most beautiful woman I have ever seen." Lightly, he ran his hand up Gillian's right arm, cupping it around the elbow and gently pulling her to him.

"You are?" The fabric of his shirt was warm beneath her fingertips. Suddenly it was hard for Gillian to breathe.

"Yes, silly girl, I am," he said playfully. "Surely you know by now that I think you're adorable." The arm he held around her pulled Gillian a fraction closer.

190

She shook her head, unable to speak.

"Gillian!" Max reached up with his free hand and gently caressed the slope of her cheek. "You *are* beautiful, you know. And brilliant. And funny. And brave." His eyes searched hers, as if trying to look into her soul. "I'm very proud of you. You've grown so much. There's nothing I've wanted more than to see you come to the place you are today. I've thought about you for years."

"You have?" Gillian whispered. His words echoed in her ears, but she could not bring herself to believe them. "I was sure you forgot about me long ago."

"Forget you?" Max shook his head firmly. "Not likely. I'm not sure how you did it, but even then you captured my heart." He regarded her seriously. "Oh no. I never forgot. I worried about you back then. You seemed lost, not sure what to believe. I've prayed for you ever since I left." Gillian caught her breath at this. "Not every day," he admitted a bit sheepishly. "But I had you written on my list of people who I wanted to see come to the Lord. I wasn't sure if I would ever see you again, ever know what happened to you. But I always cared about you, Gillian. I think I felt something special for you, even way back then.

"Of course," he said with a grin, "it wasn't anything like *this.*"

"And what is 'this'?" Gillian had to know, though she was almost afraid to ask.

"Well, this is *attraction* for one thing, that's for sure!" Max lifted one hand and ran it lovingly through the softness of her hair. Gillian closed her eyes, reveling in the sensation of being in Max's arms at last. "This is something very powerful. Something...kind of scary." His voice shook, ever so slightly. "And it's something that feels an awful lot like love."

At the word *love,* Gillian's head began to swim. Feeling light-headed, she finally allowed herself to relax against him, leaning in just as Max tipped his head toward hers and captured her lips in a brief, yet tender kiss.

A moment later, he pulled gently away, gazing into her soul. The look he gave her as he stepped back was clearly one of adoration. And the hand that claimed hers said as much through its touch as if he had spoken on a loudspeaker—communicating reassurance and devotion throughout the entire walk back to campus.

As she sat at the busy sidewalk café, watching business workers and college students stroll by, Gillian smiled at the memory and chewed another forkful of salad greens. She was still replaying the scene when a rich-timbered voice broke into her musings.

"Hey there, gorgeous."

She glanced up in surprise, then broke into a huge smile. "Max! What are you doing here? I thought you had a meeting."

"I did, but it got out early, so I thought I'd join you." He reached out with lightning-quick fingers and snagged a sliver of radish from her salad, which he immediately popped into his mouth.

"You got out of a *meeting* early? Wow. I guess I *do* believe in miracles," she quipped.

Max grinned. "So do I. *You*, for one." He dropped a quick kiss onto her cheek, then settled himself across from her at the table.

"Want some?" she asked, pushing her plate toward him.

"Nah, I'll get my own. What's good?" his eyes scanned the menu.

"Everything," Gillian assured him. The downtown restaurant was a local favorite. "Try the deep-dish chicken pot pie...or the sweet-and-sour pork kabobs." Ultimately, Max selected a tantalizing pineapple-beef stir-fry. Once the waitress had taken his order, he settled back against the chair and fixed his eyes on Gillian.

"And just what are you looking at?" she asked, fork poised midair.

Max smiled. "Just looking, that's all."

"Are you going to do that the entire time I eat?"

"Probably."

Gillian shrugged. "Suit yourself." But her face flushed with a mixture of embarrassment and pleasure.

"Thank you." Max nodded graciously. "Looking at you *does* suit me." He gave her a wink. "We're at a good place in our relationship, Gillian," he assured her. "Everyone should be so lucky."

"Yeah." The thought made her nervous. She hadn't done anything to deserve this, and it still felt terribly fragile. She gave a little frown.

"Are you all packed?" he said, referring to her trip to Palomar Observatory.

Gillian nodded. "More or less," she mumbled around a mouthful of food, then took a long drink of water. "But I don't know that I'm looking forward to it, exactly."

"Why not? Two weeks ago, you were thrilled."

"I know," Gillian mumbled unhappily. "But that was when the trip was two weeks away. Now it's here." She shuddered at the prospect of her 5:30 wake-up call the next day. "I'm looking forward to the work. It's just that…well, I'm finally getting used to being around you."

"Thanks." Max gave her a sarcastic smile.

"Stop it," she scolded fondly. "You know what I mean."

His expression grew serious. "No. I don't," he said soberly. "Tell me."

Gillian glanced around nervously. Tell him? *Tell him* that leaving him—even for two weeks—would be sheer torture? Tell him she was afraid that he'd realize after she was gone that he didn't really love her? Tell him that for once she was starting to feel a sense of peace, of stability, of *safety* in her life that she was terrified to disrupt?

As far back as she could remember, Gillian had longed for more than she had…more attention from her father, more love, more security. Finally, she had come to a place where she was no longer consumed by her loneliness. Traveling by herself, away from Max's comfortable presence and reassuring words about her walk with God, was the most threatening thing she could imagine. Talking about those fears, however, placed a close second.

It wasn't that she didn't trust Max to be understanding. It was simply that she felt—irrationally, she realized—that if she didn't speak the words, somehow they would not come true. But as Max held her gaze with his gentle blue eyes, Gillian knew that she could not hold back the truth. If there was anyone she could trust, it was Max. And if she was ever going to learn how to let herself love someone, now was the time.

"The thing is…" she began timidly, "I don't really want to leave Princeton right now."

Max caught her gaze and held it. "Why?"

Gillian felt her hands begin to tremble. Carefully, she laid down her fork. "I feel safe right now," she admitted, her words soft and low. "I like the way the last few weeks have been. I've…I've liked spending time with you, and…"

"And?" Max never looked away, not even for a moment.

"And…I'm going to miss you." Max's eyes gleamed. Gillian breathed a deep sigh. There. She'd said it. Relief washed over her.

"I'm going to miss you, too," he said with feeling. But as he reached across the table to squeeze her fingers, the old demons of fear and doubt returned, and Gillian could not help but feel that what they were experiencing was too good to last.

She let her fingers slip from his grasp. "What are you going to do while I'm gone?" she asked brightly, forcing her attention back to the plate before her.

"We-ell," Max said slowly, a smile beginning to spread across his features. "I wasn't sure until last night, but I think I've come up with a plan to keep me busy."

"Nothing *too* fun, I hope?" Gillian said lightheartedly, but something about his words made her feel uneasy.

"Oh no. Nothing big," Max laughed. But he looked nervous, as if he was afraid she might not like what he was about to say. "I'm just going to Rome," he said casually.

Gillian's fork clattered to her plate. The world around them seemed to fade away and disappear. She could see only Max. "To...Rome?" She searched his eyes. He had to be kidding.

"Yeah," he said easily. "Why? What's the matter?" He smiled politely at the waitress who came and set his pineapple-beef stir-fry in front of him. Gillian waited impatiently as the woman laid out an extra set of silverware for Max. He thanked her as she turned to go, then threw a glance back at Gillian.

"What is it, Gilly? Are you bummed I didn't wait until you could come, too?" he asked kindly. "You'll have plenty of opportunity to go later. I've been thinking about heading back there at the end of the school year."

A cold chill settled over Gillian. She tried to speak, failed, then licked her dry lips and tried again. "You...what?" She could feel the blood rushing to her head as fear-driven adrenaline kicked in.

"Plan to go back. I have a lot of friends there that I miss." Max stuffed a huge bite of red pepper and juicy beef into his mouth. Gillian stared at him. "What?" he mumbled around the food in his mouth. "Are you really surprised? I was there for several years, you know. I miss them a lot more than I thought I would. I've been thinking about it for a while, and—"

"And just when were you going to fill me in on your little

195

plan?" Gillian spat out bitterly. "Or maybe you weren't going to tell me at all? Maybe—"

Max froze, his mouth still full of food. "Gi—?" He tried to speak, swallowed hard, then tried again. "Are you all right? Wha—?"

She didn't even slow down. "I suppose you were just going to call and tell my dad and let him give me the news?"

He shook his head helplessly. "Gillian, you're going to have to give me a clue, here. I have no idea what you're—"

"'That's right, Gilly,'" she imitated her father's booming voice. "'Max is leaving. Oh, he didn't tell you? Hm. That's a shame.'" Max's eyes opened wide as understanding dawned on him. "Well, that's life," she continued bitterly. "Maybe you can stop by and leave me a telescope, or some old binoculars or something, before you go, and make everything okay."

"Gilly, please," Max pleaded. His face had gone white beneath his pale summer tan. "I had no idea. Really. I didn't realize that it hurt you so much when I—"

"Don't worry about it, Max," Gillian said coolly, trying to avoid his gaze. She stood, kicking her chair back, and grabbed her slim black purse. "I survived when you left before. I can live through it again. Go ahead and make your plans. Go back to Rome. I just wish you would have told me before I...before I—"

"Gillian, come on now. Stop this. Just sit down, and we'll discuss this reasonably, like two rational adults," he urged.

"No! I *won't* discuss this with you. I can't, Max. Don't you see?" She was quite hysterical now, and the other patrons in the restaurant had started staring at them. Gillian rambled on, oblivious to their looks. "I didn't want to like you again, but now I have...and I just can't *do this*. I don't want to hear about how you like me, but that God has opened a door for you someplace else. I don't want to pretend everything is going to

196

be okay, that we'll visit each other—we'll write. That's not gonna happen. It's ridiculous."

"Yes," Max said heavily. He was clearly angry now. He tried once more, nodding for Gillian to reclaim her empty seat. "This *is* ridiculous. If you would just—"

"No, Max. Please. Just forget this ever happened, okay? For me?" She gave him a pointed stare. "It's the only thing I've ever asked."

Gillian turned away, and with tears streaming from her eyes, rushed from the restaurant, onto the sidewalk, and away from the only man who had ever given her a glimpse of love.

Fourteen

Jesus looked at them and said, "With man this is impossible, but with God all things are possible."

MATTHEW 19:26

March 29, 1988

It's funny how things can change so fast. I remember when Mom gave me this diary, I didn't think I'd have anything to write in it. It's become a habit now, and I'm glad. It feels good to get everything down on paper, though I'm not sure it helps me make much sense of things. I can't believe I said that nothing ever happens to me. If only I'd known. That was almost one year ago, but it feels more like a hundred.

Mom and I moved to D.C. during spring break, two weeks ago today. I've talked to Dad a couple of times on the phone. I've never heard him sound sad before. It's a strange thing to hear. It probably feels weird to him, to come home at night and find no one there. Norrie still comes by during the day and makes little microwavable dinners for him. I talked to her yesterday, too. She said she had to make Dad buy all new casserole dishes. The ones he had were just too big.

School isn't so bad, really. I'm in public school for the first time. It's kind of crazy, but I like getting lost in the crowd. I'd gotten used to being on my own back in Princeton, anyway. Jenny's got a lot of friends, and I was right when I figured people would take sides. Matt

Ross made it through okay. He's dating Ginny Davis now, the head of the cheerleading squad—and if you ask me, they can have each other. His cousin Chris actually did go back to wherever he came from—Chicago, I think.

I finally broke down and told Mom what happened. Her opinion is that I made it harder on myself than it had to be. She said that in high school, everyone worries about what everyone else is thinking about them, when really those people aren't thinking anything at all—they're too busy wondering what everyone is thinking about them.

She tells me that if I hadn't given up, Jenny and I would have been fine. But there's no point in worrying about that: I stopped trying to smooth things over with Jenny months ago. By the time school started, we were actually avoiding each other. Maybe things would have been better if I'd given it another chance. Then again, maybe not. Maybe the other girls didn't hate me as much as I thought. I guess it doesn't matter now. I mostly keep to myself. Things are easier this way. I'm not hurting anybody, and no one's hurting me.

Mom told me last week that I have her permission to go out on dates now. She's been feeling pretty bad about dragging me away from Princeton. Apparently this is supposed to make the transition easier for me. I didn't know how to tell her I have no desire to go out with anybody.

Mom wants me to start going to church with her, too, but I think I'm gonna pass. Every time I've ever gone before, people talk about being open and involved and loving. It's very sentimental, and I just don't think I'm up to it. Back in Princeton, I thought every once in a while about ignoring Dad's grumbling and going to church. Especially after Max started talking about God. I'd never thought that Christianity was so logical before. I always thought it was anti-science.

It's not really the logic part that bothers me, though. It's just that it feels too hard to try. I don't like the way my life is right now. But at least I know how to deal with it. I'm not ready to rock that boat just yet. Mom talks about how loving everybody is at the church, but I don't want anyone to say they want to love me. Not if it isn't going to last.

Last night I unpacked my telescope and sat outside, trying to look at the stars. It's not easy here. The city lights are too bright. Stars that were clear in New Jersey are pale here, and some of them I can't even see. Draco the Dragon was almost invisible. I was able to pick out a few of my favorites, though...Orion and his belt; the Great Bear; Ursa Major; and of course, Betelgeuse. I still remember the look on my dad's face when I was five years old and I asked him why they named a star after bug guts.

It helps to know that the stars here are the same ones we had in Jersey, even if they aren't as bright. Sometimes it feels funny, looking into the eyepiece of Max's telescope. I never forget that it was his. Sometimes I get the funny feeling that when I look into it, I'm going to see into the past, see something he used to see. Of course, that doesn't happen. But it's fun to imagine that it could.

I've used Max's telescope a lot during the last six months. Dad looked at me real funny the first time he caught me carrying it outside. I'm sure he wondered where it came from and why I wasn't using the one he gave me. But when he opened his mouth to say something, I just gave him a really hard look, and for the first time since I can remember, he snapped his mouth shut and let me be.

Maybe arguing with Mom had taken some of the fight out of him. They argued about everything, not just Dad's work schedule and Mom's religion, during those last few months. Once the big issues became too big to handle, I guess everything else fell apart, too. I don't understand why they had to separate, though. Things have been like this for years, it's nothing new. Mom just said one day that she'd had enough, that she was moving to Washington. No one ever asked me what I thought, whether I wanted to go. It was as if there wasn't any question about me going with Mom. Dad and I haven't gotten along in years. I guess that's why it feels so odd to miss him so much.

After all these years of fighting Dad, it's strange that I'm able to look at the stars and love them again. I think about him when I do. I know that he's looking at them, too, though not in the same way. Where I see mystery and light, he sees radar readings and photometric plots. It's not the same, but it's not exactly different, either. I feel closer to Dad during those times than I have in years.

Sometimes when I'm looking up, I wonder, too, if Max is watching the same sky. It tears me up inside that I never said good-bye. But good-byes are hard. Maybe for some people the only way through them is not to say them at all.

It makes it hard for me to even want to say hello.

September 19, 1997

Gillian's hand slipped gently across the soft red leather cover of the volume she cradled in her lap. Two days after she had made her decision to follow God, Max had given her the Bible as a gift, saying simply: "I can't think of anything more worth celebrating." Inside the front cover, he had scribbled upon one of the slippery white pages:

> To Gilly—
> Today is just the beginning. May God's love and mercies fill your soul from now until the ends of the earth...and into the eternity that lies beyond the stars.
> Love,
> Max

Love...Max. The words blurred before her eyes, turning into nothing but a murky cloud of ink. If only she could hear him say it one more time. *"This is something very powerful. Something...that feels an awful lot like love."* Gillian had never known before what it felt like to be in love. She'd caught a taste of it when she was a teenager, the first time Max had stolen her heart. But that was nothing like the emotions that now filled her heart. It was different to know him, to love him as an equal and not as a child. It was different, knowing they truly *could* be together and praying that one day that dream would come true.

Never before had anyone cared so deeply for her and the state of her soul. After he had given Gillian the Bible and had watched her leaf through it helplessly, he had taken it upon himself to show her where his favorite verses were and walked her through her initial confusion concerning the book's structure, which she soon discovered was more understandable than it appeared.

At his suggestion, she had chosen to begin her studies with the Gospel accounts. Some nights, she read just a few verses. Other times, she pored over entire chapters. Before long she was meeting Christ face-to-face, discovering amazing truths about the faith she had embraced...truths concerning God's love for her, the plan he had for her life. It was still hard to believe it was all real, but Gillian knew that this time—even during those moments when her doubts returned—she would not walk away. She could not afford to.

Especially now.

Gillian kicked back onto the bright yellow couch and groaned. Her heart ached, her soul hurt...*everything* about her hurt. Even *she* was appalled at the way she had behaved that afternoon. Angry, out of control, bitter...she had lashed out at Max venomously. Not exactly the picture of spiritual virtue...or the kind of woman he would want to love. And now, she had ruined everything. Max was a gracious man, but there were limits to what even *he* could withstand. Before she stormed away from the restaurant, Gillian had seen through her tears the hard lines of Max's face, had heard the angry finality in his voice when he ordered her to sit back down and discuss the situation rationally. His tolerance level was high, but finally she had pushed Max Bishop over the top.

I didn't do it on purpose, she thought defensively. *I said what I felt.* Her response to Max's news had been a natural reaction, an instinctive move to extricate herself from the most painful situation she could imagine. Losing Max at all would be agonizing enough. Losing him *slowly* would be pure torture. She could not continue to date him, to allow herself the luxury of his company and his touch. Gillian hardly knew how she could bear to work beside him, growing to love him more with every moment, each day knowing that soon Max would leave her again.

Of course, Max had not yet expressed his decision to leave…although if that decision had been in question before their argument, it most certainly was settled in his heart by now. Surely Max would not want to be with her anymore. Gillian didn't even want to be with herself.

She opened the book sitting across her knees and started to flip forward to the book of Luke but paused as the pages fell open to a passage she had highlighted in Matthew 21, several weeks before.

He said to his disciples, "Why are you so afraid? Do you still have no faith?"

A knot tightened in Gillian's stomach as she read the words a second time…then another. Jesus might as well have been speaking to her. In the past month, her fears had subsided to a certain degree. But now, faced with the prospect of losing Max, her feelings of panic and loneliness were quickly rising…and growing. She closed her eyes and prayed,

Lord, please help me. I feel like I'm losing it, here. Max told me today that he's thinking about leaving Princeton again, and I went off the deep end. I screamed and yelled, made a whole big scene. Max

didn't deserve that. I'm sure you couldn't have been pleased. Her prayer was silent, but the words tumbled through her mind even faster than she could speak them.

I know you want me to have faith, God. But I am afraid. Afraid of losing Max, afraid of failing you…afraid of never having another relationship, of any kind, that will last longer than a month or two….

Gillian wrapped her arms around herself and pulled them close, craving any tiny measure of comfort she could receive.

I'm sorry I've been so stubborn. Please help me to find some kind of peace. I want to trust you, but I can't imagine how you could make any good come out of this situation, Lord. Still, I'll be happy if you do. And I believe that you can, even if I can't see it.

She thought hard for a moment, then squinted her eyes up tight and offered up one last plea: *God, I feel like what I said to Max is true. I can't handle it if he's going to go away. I'm afraid of leaving my heart open and then losing him.* The floodgates were open now, and the words came easily. *But at the same time, I don't want to give up completely, even though that's what I've always wanted to do before. I love him, Lord. I really love him. If you have someone else for him, I guess there's nothing I can do about that. But I want you to know that I do care for him, more than I've ever cared for anyone before, even though I never told him so. I'm really glad I had him in my life, and I want to thank you for that. If I have to let him go, I'll try. I'll need your help to get through it, Lord, but I'll try. Still, I can't help but ask—because I'm finally learning that you want me to bring my dreams to you—if there's any possibility of getting one last chance, Lord, I'd be so grateful. All I ask is one more chance—*

Her lips were still moving, silently, when the front screen door swung open wide and slammed shut with a bang. Gillian opened her eyes to see Bridget stepping in from the sunshine. As usual, her eyes narrowed slightly at the sight of Gillian, but the look passed quickly, and soon her face was devoid of emotion.

"Hi, Gillian," she said casually and dropped her backpack to the floor. Gillian quickly uttered a silent *Amen* and gave her roommate a curious look. Bridget's entrance at that particular moment in time was not especially remarkable. It was true that she nearly always arrived home much later in the day. But it wasn't unheard of for her to take the afternoon off. Maybe class had been canceled; perhaps she had a stomachache. Still, Gillian could not help but wonder at the timing. Hadn't she just prayed for one more chance? Of course, she had been talking about Max and was sure that God knew it. After her behavior that day, such a reprieve didn't seem likely. Perhaps God was offering her a new beginning with Bridget instead.

She cleared her throat loudly, as if she were preparing to speak before a hall of VFW veterans. "Hey, Bridget," she said brightly, addressing the woman in her warmest tone. "How'd your day go?"

Bridget gave her an odd stare. "Fine," she said quickly, but not rudely, and proceeded to make a beeline through the living room.

"Uh...hey, Bridget?" Gillian called after her, wondering how she could get her roommate to stop and talk.

The woman hesitated. "Yeah?" She stood with one hand on her denim-skirted hip. Her white blouse was limp and hung heavily against her skin. She looked tired. Her tone did not invite casual conversation. If Gillian wanted to talk with Bridget about the situation, she was just going to have to cut to the chase.

"Um, I feel like I really need to talk to you," Gillian said timidly. She looked into Bridget's brown doe eyes and felt a pang in her heart at the blatant mistrust she read there.

"What about?" Bridget asked uneasily.

"Well, it's about the whole Max thing," Gillian admitted, then raised one hand as Bridget opened her mouth to protest. "I know, I know, we've covered this already, but I still feel terrible about it, and I think there are some things I need to say. You may not need to go over this again, but I do, and I'd really appreciate it if you'd let me talk about it with you."

Bridget studied her warily, then cautiously moved back into the living room. She perched herself on the edge of the well-worn red armchair, as if prepared at any moment to take flight. She said nothing, simply waited for Gillian to speak.

Bridget obviously didn't want to sit around and gab, so Gillian began to speak, "I don't know exactly what to say here, Bridget," she admitted, standing awkwardly at the woman's side. "I think I've apologized, but it doesn't seem like that's enough. I know you're still mad at me, you probably hate me…and honestly, I understand." The longer she stood there, trying to connect with the unresponsive statue that was Bridget, the more desperate for forgiveness she felt. "I didn't at first. I couldn't see anything, really, except the fact that I was mad, too. I kind of get that way, you know? Defensive. But I know you trusted me, and I know I let you down. I don't know how to fix that."

"I don't know if you can," Bridget said honestly.

"Yeah." Gillian relaxed a bit at this first sign of real interaction. "I know. Like I said, I don't know what to tell you. My intention never was to hurt you." She tried to think of what else to say. It wasn't easy. Normally, it was her practice just to let broken relationships slip away. She hadn't extended herself in an attempt to salvage one since she was a child. "I don't know…I just went sort of crazy when Max got here," she tried to explain, hoping Bridget would somehow understand.

"He was…he was the first guy I ever felt anything for, and the last one I ever believed in. I never felt very loved by my dad, but Max at least made me feel special for a while. He treated me like I was important and valuable. After he left, I was all mixed up inside." Gillian noticed that Bridget's expression had softened slightly, and she blushed at the pity she thought she saw there. She started to turn away. "I guess this is *way* more information than you want or need about my life, so I'll just—"

"No, it's not," Bridget said clearly.

"What?" Gillian stopped and gave her a strange look. "It's not?"

"No." Bridget's short curls danced as she swung her head from side to side. "Do you realize that's the first time you told me anything personal—I mean *really* personal about your life?"

"No." Gillian stared at her. "I'm sure it's not."

"*Gillian,*" her roommate sighed in exasperation. "It *is*. I think you mentioned once that your parents were separated. And one time when Pam and I were grilling you about your track record with guys you mumbled something about getting burned when you were younger. That is *not* the same as sharing on a personal level."

"I guess you're right," Gillian admitted reluctantly.

"Gillian, despite what you think, I really don't hate you," Bridget said sadly, her stone-faced facade finally broken. "I never hated you. Not for a minute. I liked you a *lot*. That's why I felt so bad when I thought you'd turned on me."

"Oh, Bridget!" The sting of hot tears came to her eyes. "I never meant to turn on you. And I wasn't trying to keep Max for myself, honestly I wasn't!"

"I know," Bridget said, and she sounded as if she meant it. "But can you see why I would feel that way?"

"Of course I can. But can't you see that I—"

"Gillian." The look in Bridget's eyes was considerably less than fond. "You said you didn't know what else to do to make things better. Do you want me to tell you?"

She could see that Bridget was serious. "Yes, I do."

"If you want me to forgive you, then *ask* me to forgive you. Don't just keep on telling me your side of the story. If you know that you did something wrong, then apologize and leave it at that. I feel like you keep waiting for me to say it was okay. It *wasn't* okay. But that doesn't mean I won't forgive you."

Suddenly, Gillian felt as though a massive weight had been lifted from her shoulders. Something miraculous was occurring. Bridget was actually *talking* to her. They were connecting. Perhaps—no, *unquestionably*—more than they ever had before. Here, at last, was the hope she feared she'd lost. "Bridget, I *am* sorry about what happened," she said honestly. "It doesn't matter what my intentions were. I handled things poorly. I hurt you, and I was wrong. Please," she said as meaningfully as she could, "would you forgive me?"

The emotional wall crashed to the ground. Brown eyes brimming, Bridget stood and threw her arms around Gillian's shoulders. "Of course I forgive you, Gil," she sniffed. "All you ever had to do was ask." Gillian found herself wrapping both arms around Bridget and hugging her, too. Moments later, the two collapsed side-by-side on the couch. Both were exhausted from crying, but it was a good exhaustion, and Gillian's soul felt lighter.

"You know," Bridget said after several minutes, "I really need to ask your forgiveness, too."

"You do?" Gillian looked at her in wonder. Then she felt a wave of amazement over the fact that she actually felt surprised. Up until several minutes earlier, she had been harboring a grudge against Bridget. In the process of humbling herself before her roommate, her own grievances had been forgotten.

"Yeah, I do," Bridget was saying. "I pushed you pretty hard, and there were a couple of times when I was pretty nasty. I'm sorry, Gil. I had no right to act that way."

"All's forgiven." Gillian smiled and impulsively reached out and gave her another quick hug.

"So..." Bridget said cheerfully, the awkward moment past, "What are you doing tonight? You wanna go grab a latté?" She interrupted herself. "No, probably not. I suppose you're going out with Max again?" Gillian's face fell. "What? What did I say?" she asked anxiously.

Before her conversion, Gillian would have brushed the question aside and left it at that. Opening up about something so personal, so close to her heart, was foreign territory to her. But something had changed in Gillian. It was as if the buds of trust were opening in her for the first time since she was sixteen. Within minutes, she had managed to explain to Bridget, through her tears, that she and Max had fought—though she did not go into detail concerning the specifics of the argument—that she was terrified of losing him, and that she had never been so miserable in all her life.

As the story unfolded, Bridget sat at Gillian's side without saying a word, patting her back and murmuring comforting phrases.

"I don't know what to tell you," Bridget confessed after she had finished. Gillian continued sniffling into a white tissue from a cardboard box on the end table. "It sounds like you have a lot to think about. I'm probably not the best person to advise you," she said honestly. "But...there's one thing I *can* do." She smiled eagerly, an action that caused her whole face to light up.

"What's that?" Gillian asked as she grabbed two more tissues.

At just that moment, the front door opened once more. After two steps, Pam froze just inside the threshold and stared at the two women on the couch, her eyes grazing over Gillian first, then the pile of wadded-up tissues, and finally resting on Bridget.

"Having a party?" she quipped dryly.

"*No,*" said Bridget indignantly, "but we *are* going out on the town. You, too, Pam."

"What?" Gillian turned to her, openmouthed. "We are?"

"We are?" Pam repeated, in a tone that said, "If you're going to include me in your little plans, you'd better explain yourself, missy."

"We *are,*" Bridget repeated firmly. She laid one hand on Gillian's arm. "We can't make your problems go away, but we can at least try to help you forget about them for a little while."

"But, Bridget, I don't think I can forget about anything," Gillian said heavily. "Besides, I have to get up early. I just want to go to my room and—"

"And what? Mope?" Bridget flicked her hand in the air in a dismissive gesture. "You've got two weeks to do that. You're leaving in the morning, and I want you to remember that you've got something good to come home to. *Your friends,*" she said pointedly, reaching out and patting her on the knee. "Don't worry about getting up early; we'll make sure you're not out too late."

By now, Pam was ready to jump on the bandwagon. "Why not, Gil?" she suggested, looking clearly relieved that the two had finally resolved their differences. "It's your last night home, let's go paint the town." She stepped into the living room and planted herself in the red armchair.

"Besides," Bridget jumped in, "if you're having a hard time right now, what you need is to be around your girlfriends."

Those words, more than any others, were the ones that made the decision for her. The last thing Gillian wanted was to have to spend the night being cheerful. But she'd never had friends before that she could turn to in times of crisis. It was a dangling carrot too appetizing to resist.

"Do I have to be in a good mood?" she grumbled.

"Nope," Bridget promised. "You can do anything you want. We'll let you pick the movie, the restaurant. I'll even buy you a big, sticky piece of German chocolate cake."

"I don't think I want chocolate cake," Gillian told her.

Her two roommates stared at each other in horror. "Not want chocolate?" Pam said, as if she could not believe she'd heard the words.

Bridget shook her head sadly and felt Gillian's forehead for a fever, like a sick child. "Poor thing," she sympathized. "You must be even worse off than I thought. Oh, well. More cake for me!"

Though the feelings of loss still wracked her soul, Gillian managed to muster a weak smile at the realization of how far the two of them had just come. The thought came, crazily, that Max would be proud of Gillian if he knew.... He would tell her she was growing, that God was working in her heart. It was at that moment that the truth behind the words Max once spoke hit Gillian with tremendous force:

"With God, all things are possible."

She smiled.

Apparently, even the impossible.

Fifteen

I will not let thee go.
I hold thee by too many bands;
Thou sayest farewell, and lo!
I have thee by the hands,
And will not let thee go.

ROBERT BRIDGES, *I WILL NOT LET THEE GO*

January 7, 1989

Had a great time up in Princeton this weekend. With Dad's schedule being so busy and all, I don't get up there half as much as I'd like. Virginia and D.C. are nice, too, but it's just not the same as New Jersey. Dad had me talk to one of the guys in the admissions office. Normally, they don't work weekends, I'm sure. But Dad's still got a lot of clout. It actually felt pretty good being back on campus. As a kid, I always thought I would end up going to school there. I remember wandering around feeling like such a child. I don't feel like a child anymore.

As we left Admissions, Dad told me that he wanted to head over to his office to pick up some papers he'd left there the day before. Dad's getting a little scatterbrained these days. Maybe it's age, I don't know. It could be something else. He hasn't been the same since Mom left, I've noticed. And I'm not the only one.

Mom told me last month that Dad got into a bit of trouble with the head honchos at the university. I don't know how she knew. I guess Dad must have told her. Anyway, it seems that Dad's performance has suffered a little bit over the last year. I've seen it a little in

213

talking with him. His mind isn't as sharp, that's for sure. Apparently, his classes aren't filling up quite as quickly anymore, and I heard he got in trouble for turning in his grades late. Dad always said, if there's one thing universities take seriously, besides money, it's grades.

So Dad and I stopped by the office where we ran into Dr. Randall. I hadn't seen him in years—not since before Mom and I moved, I think. Not that I ever saw him much before. He and Dad have always been pretty competitive. Theirs is kind of a love-hate friendship. Anyway, we spent a few minutes catching up, then he asked Dad if he'd heard about the guy from Harvard.

"Who?" Dad asked.

"You know. Oh, I forget his name. Wait, it's around here some-where...." I didn't think much about it. I don't know who the professors are over at Harvard, and I really couldn't care less. But it turned out it wasn't a teacher, after all.

"Here it is," Randall said. "Look!" He held it out to my father. Dad's face turned bright red. I looked over his shoulder.

And there it was, some scientific abstract about multidimensional theories in cosmology, written by a doctor named Zeller, or Zellum, or something. But right underneath Zeller's name, as a special honor, they had printed the name of the graduate student who assisted him in his work:

Maxwell Bishop.

Dad looked like he'd swallowed a goldfish. Ol' Randall looked pretty smug. I don't know that I felt anything at first. Crushes are strange things. The year after I met Max, I thought about him a lot. I needed to. It was a hard year, and I didn't have much else that made me feel good. Not that missing him felt good. It was agony, pure and simple. I know, I know...every girl obsesses about her first crush for a while. But this crush dragged on for a long time, even after he was gone.

The truth is, I still think about Max sometimes. Mostly when I'm lonely. It feels like a cruel trick, to find someone I think I could care about, no, that I actually did care about, and to have him snatched away.

I don't really have reason to complain, though. I have a pretty good life. I have my entire college experience ahead of me. My relationship with my parents may not be the best in the world, but at least it's improving. And of course, I've got the stars…and I always will.

That's right, I finally decided on a major. My counselor at school told me I had a year or more to choose one, but Dad was insistent. He was speechless when I told him I was going for astrophysics. I suppose I could have chosen math or general physics and kept my career plans to myself. But what would have been the point of that? I'm the one who would have suffered most, not Dad. Besides, I don't feel so much like punishing him anymore. After all, he is the one who gave me a love for the stars in the first place. At least I have that to thank him for. It feels good to finally be able to say that. It took me a long time to get over blaming him for losing Max.

I suspect I may still think about Max too much. Oh, I don't day-dream about him, really. But he's always there, just under the surface of my memory…when I'm out on a date, when I'm thinking about the future and all that lies ahead. I remember how kind Max was to me, how compassionate and understanding. I remember the way he stood up to my dad and made his scientific theories palatable even to my mother. I remember his passion for his studies, his work, his future…even his God. It makes it hard to put much effort into dating guys who take me to kickboxing movies and talk about souping up their Trans-Ams. I always thought I'd get married someday, but I'm not sure I believe it anymore.

I want a family, though. Deep inside, there's a part of me that dreams about having a baby, pushing a tricycle, being a Den Mother. I picture lazy Saturday mornings filled with crossword puzzles and coffee…I see my husband and me painting the house together. I imagine lying out in the backyard, pointing up at the sky above, and *telling my own daughter or son about the star made of bug guts. It's a "Hi, honey, I'm home" kind of dream.*

I just have a hard time picturing the man who calls me "Honey."

September 20, 1997

Gillian yawned and stretched, wishing for the umpteenth time that she had taken the time to program her roommate's automatic coffeemaker the night before. Five-thirty had come all too early this morning…this in spite of the fact that she hadn't slept a wink. She supposed she owed Bridget and Pam a debt of gratitude. If they hadn't taken her out the night before, she probably would have lain awake, staring at her plaster ceiling for more than ten hours instead of a mere six and a half.

Grumpily, she glared at the line that snaked ahead of her up to the airline ticket counter. It wouldn't be so bad, standing here, she thought, if I didn't really need a cup of coffee. She craved caffeine. Unlike Bridget, Gillian could not depend on java alone to get her going in the morning. She needed food, too. Today, she'd had neither, and as a result, she was feeling incredibly crabby.

Except…that wasn't exactly true, and she knew it. The cause of her distress was less physiological than it was emotional. When she'd come home last night, the first thing she'd done was check the answering machine for messages, but none were left. Clearly, Max didn't want to talk to her. But, then, why was that a surprise?

In an attempt to draw her mind away from thoughts of Max, she focused on a nearby monitor, trying to read the arrival and departure times, but there wasn't any point in that. Nothing had worked the night before, nothing was going to work now. Pam and Bridget had been real troopers, taking her out for dinner and a comedy film—"No romances allowed," Bridget had ordered as she scanned the paper's movie section—

then stuffing her with air-cooked movie-theater popcorn.

Though the other two women had enjoyed the movie, Gillian hadn't let out so much as a giggle. She couldn't even remember the basic plot an hour afterward; that was how much attention she had been paying. Her roommates were understanding, though, and even sweet about it throughout the entire evening. Conversation at dinner had been light, and Pam and Bridget had carried Gillian's portion of it. Her silence at the theater was clearly noticed, but not commented upon. And after the movie, the women had taken her at her word when she said she wanted to go home. Gillian knew that they hadn't expected to actually cheer her up; they just wanted her to know that she wasn't alone. And for that, she truly was thankful.

As the line began to slither forward, Gillian grabbed her bags and moved ahead. At least they were moving. That was something.

Despite her heavy eyes, her irritation, and her growling stomach, time eventually passed, and she was able to check in with twenty-five minutes to spare before boarding. A grim-looking airline worker checked her large suitcase while a cheerful ticket agent handed Gillian her boarding pass. After a brief stop at a concourse coffee stand, she found herself sitting in one of the rows of plastic seats near the gate: carry-on bag at her feet, *café au lait* and sugar-free bran muffin in hand. As she waited, she peeled back the paper of her breakfast, which under normal circumstances would have been a treat. But this morning it tasted like sawdust.

Gillian washed the muffin down with coffee, enjoying the comforting feel of it as it eased down her throat. She needed the liquid's warmth—her short-sleeved willow-green T-shirt, loose-fitting jeans, and white canvas sneakers were perfect for a hot southern California climate but not an air-conditioned airport terminal.

She stared out the waiting-area window at the airplane that would soon carry her three thousand miles away from the man she loved. Flight attendants and pilots slipped through a door clearly designated for airport personnel. As she waited for the gate to open, feelings of regret settled over her, and her heart was filled with doubt.

Had she done the right thing in revealing her feelings to Max? It was obvious that she had handled the situation poorly, ranting like a lunatic...but were her feelings valid? Gillian played the argument over and over again in her mind, just as she had hundreds of times the night before. Her conclusion was the same every time. There was no way around it. There was nothing Max could have said that would have calmed her. She had been completely out of control. She couldn't justify herself by saying it had been a natural expression of emotions. The truth was, she hadn't expressed a single emotion other than anger, and even that had been communicated in a less than healthy manner. She could not expect Max to forgive her for such an outburst.

Her conversation with Bridget had had a tremendous impact on her, however. Following a full night of soul-searching, she knew she had to at least try to make peace with Max. After listening to Bridget's frank advice, Gillian understood that it was possible to work through conflicts. Max might not want to be close to her anymore, but at least she could ask him for his forgiveness. It might not bring him back, but it could at least help to soften his anger and add some closure to the whole ordeal.

She was licking dry bran crumbs from her fingers when the flight attendant informed the crowd that the boarding of their flight would begin.

"At this time we would like to begin seating all passengers with small children and those requiring special assistance," the perky brunette announced.

I wonder if that includes mental and emotional assistance, Gillian thought sarcastically. She had tipped her head back and was letting the last bit of coffee dribble into her mouth when she noticed the figure standing over her. The sight of him nearly caused her to spit the liquid out again. Gillian choked and swallowed hard and coughed once more, while he stood patiently waiting for her to compose herself.

"Max! What are you *doing* here?" she finally managed. Her heart beat heavily within her chest.

His clothes—stone-washed jeans and a crazy, navy-blue-flowered pseudo-Hawaiian shirt—were wrinkled, just as they had been the last time he'd been too preoccupied to plug in an iron. "I'm heading out to Palomar Mountain," he said simply, indicating the carry-on bag at his side. Gillian stared at him, not understanding.

"Does this mean the school isn't sending me, after all? Do you want—? Am I supposed to give you my ticket? Am I—" Gillian's skin turned pale as she made the connection. "Oh *no*. Does this mean I'm off the project?" She felt sickened that her tantrum might have lost her the best job she'd ever gotten. But hadn't she been thinking of the same possibility herself? If her relationship with Max was over, it would be nearly impossible to work together...even if it was just through the end of the school year. She had already decided that she would give Ed a call about the whole thing before she returned.

Max shook his head at her reaction. "No, of course not, silly. You're not off of anything." His face and voice still betrayed nothing.

She could not believe that he was actually standing there. "But you just said—"

"Look, we'll get to what I just said in a minute, okay?" he said firmly. "But right now, there are a few things I want to say to you."

"O-kay," she agreed. Her heart kept its wild cadence.

There was an empty seat in Gillian's row, but Max remained standing and quickly began to pace. "You know, you rushed off yesterday without even giving me a chance to say a word," he said roughly, wasting no time in getting to the point.

"I know, Max," Gillian murmured unhappily. "I'm sorry." Here it was. Max's good-bye speech. She had known all along it would come to this.

"Do you have any idea what it did to me, to see you all broken up like that?" he said, his voice thick with emotion. He continued to wander the aisle erratically.

The words floated in Gillian's head, as if unsure of where to land. What was Max saying? He wasn't making any sense. She struggled to grasp some small measure of understanding.

The flight attendant's voice broke in over the loudspeaker. "Could we now have all passengers assigned to rows eighteen through—"

Max planted his feet on the carpet directly in front of Gillian and held her eyes with his own. "Gilly, I've cared about you ever since you were a girl," he said frankly. "I've been attracted to you since the minute I saw you in Ed's office. And I've loved you—" He searched for words. "I think *part* of me has loved you all along, but over the past month or so, that love has grown exponentially," he said, drawing upon his extensive mathematical background to provide the analogy. "I think about you when I wake up in the morning; I think about you when I'm working—" he gave her a hint of a smile—"which is a *major* distraction, I have to tell you, especially when you're in the next room."

His words mystified her. Gillian stared at him blankly, trying to solve the mystery of what he might be trying to say. What did any of this have to do with him being at the airport? And why was he being so nice to her? Was he trying to spare her feelings?

"Max, if you're going to yell at me, it's okay," she said quietly. "Go ahead and get it over with. I've been expecting it."

But Max gave no indication of wanting to yell at her. In fact, his voice was gentle and soothing. "Gillian," he said carefully, "when you snapped yesterday, I was shocked at first, and then, yes, very angry when you wouldn't let me explain. After you rushed out of the restaurant, part of me wanted to go after you. But part of me had to cool off. Do you understand that?"

She nodded meekly.

"The thing is," he said, keeping his eyes fixed on hers, "the more I thought about it, the more I could understand." The look he gave her was increasingly tender. "Gilly, I wasn't aware of it at the time, but I know you had a hard time that year with your parents' separation. Back then, I *did* know that you had a crush on me, but I had no idea my leaving would hurt you so badly. I thought it was just a little thing, a feeling that would fade before I was even gone. But I did care about you. That's why I—"

She nodded soberly. "The telescope."

"Yeah. The telescope," Max agreed. "I wasn't trying to buy you off, Gilly, so you wouldn't be angry. I just thought it was a little something you'd remember me by." His cheeks flushed red. "I guess it was selfish, but even then I wanted to make sure you wouldn't forget me."

Gillian's eyes grew wide. As if she could ever forget Max! But why on earth was he saying all this? He didn't want to be with her anymore. How could he?

Max continued sentimentally, "Gillian, the truth of the matter is, I love you. I've loved you for a long time. And as far as my going to Rome is concerned—"

"Max, no." Gillian stood and lay one hand gently upon his arm. "I'm sorry. I had no right to get angry with you. It's none of my business what you do. I was going to call you when I got to Pasadena and apolog—"

"Gillian." The word was spoken as an admonishment, but there was amusement in his eyes. "Would you please let me finish for once?" Thoroughly chastised, she stepped back to listen. "What I'm *trying* to say," he insisted, "and what I was trying to explain *yesterday,* is that I have no intention of moving back to Rome."

Gillian shook her head. She couldn't have heard right. "You don't?"

"No, I don't. When I said I wanted to go back, I meant for a *visit.*"

She gave him a look of utter confusion. "But—but you said you were going at the end of the school year. I just assumed that the reason you wanted to go this month was to talk with them at the university about coming back. June seemed like a logical time to make a transition, to move away—"

"Do you hear yourself talking?" Max chuckled, but his laughter was not malicious. "Sweetie, I'm *not* moving away," he assured her vehemently. At the sound of the familiar endearment, Gillian felt her old fears begin to recede, ever so slightly. Slowly, a faint look of hope began to soften her features as he continued. "I'm right *here,* right now. Quite literally, in fact." He glanced around the airport terminal. Nearby, the flight crew glanced at the two of them nervously as they ushered a large group of passengers toward the plane. "And do you know why I'm here? In this airport? Getting on this plane at this unholy hour of the morning?" he asked dramatically. "Well, I'll tell you why. It's because I want to be with *you.* I'm not willing to let you go like this, and I'm willing to do whatever it takes to work through things."

"But the university said they'd only pay for one of us," Gillian protested.

"That's okay," Max assured her. "I bought the ticket myself. And I have some friends in Los Angeles I can stay with. Don't worry about any of that."

"You said you were going to Rome...." she said feebly.

"Gillian, *please.*" He looked offended that she thought he would even consider such a thing. "Did you actually expect me to fly halfway around the world when things are so unresolved between us?"

Gillian looked up at him helplessly, tears in her eyes. "Max, I didn't know! I thought you would hate me after the way I acted. How can you even want to *be* with me after that?"

Max reached out with one strong hand and caressed her face, tracing a line from her left temple to the delicate tip of her chin. "Because that wasn't you," he explained lovingly. "That's just a *part* of you, Gilly. The angry part. And believe it or not, I love the angry part, just like I love the rest of you. It might make *me* angry sometimes, too. But it's one dimension of who you are, so I accept it." With the stroke of his thumb, he wiped away one stray tear that had slipped from her eye and rolled down her cheek. "Besides, there's a lot more to you than just screaming and yelling."

Gillian flinched. "I *did* scream and yell, didn't I?" Her face turned scarlet, and she covered her mouth with one hand, giving him a look of chagrin. "Max, I've behaved horribly, and I completely mistrusted you. Can you ever forgive me?"

"Yes, I forgive you," he promised solemnly, brushing back a lock of golden hair that had fallen over her damp eyes. "But that brings up another issue."

Gillian stiffened and steeled herself for what he was about to say. "What issue is that?" she asked suspiciously.

"One of the most important issues of all: trust." Max told her simply. "You know, I can understand more or less why you jumped to the conclusion you did, Gilly, because I know a bit about your past. I've seen that trust is a major issue for you. But..." He paused and considered his words. "I have to say, I don't think most people would have jumped to the same conclusion. I think your mind twisted the words, and you believed the worst, without stopping to consider any other option." The words were harsh, but the compassion with which he spoke them softened the blow.

"Even after I tried to explain, you wouldn't hear it. It was as though there was a part of you that didn't want to believe in me, in us." He forced her to meet his eyes. "Do you think that's possible, Gilly?"

She closed her eyes and nodded wordlessly, pressing her cheek against the warmth of his hand in a gesture that expressed both a feeling of regret and a desire for comfort. Max responded to the unspoken request, untangling his fingers from her hair and enfolding her in the circle of his arms. Slowly, purposely, she allowed herself to relax within the sanctuary of his embrace.

"Gilly, I'm not ready to make you any grand proposal. Not yet," he whispered against the soft skin at her temple. "We haven't been together long enough for that. But I *can* promise you this: I am completely, one-hundred-percent committed to being here now, and to learning to love you well." He paused for a moment, giving her a chance to let his words sink in.

"Life is about choices," he said at last, "and I'm choosing to love you. I'm choosing to see where that love will go. But that's not enough. *You* have choices, too. One of them is whether or not you want to love me."

"But, Max, I do—" He silenced her with one finger to her rosy lips.

"No, no, Gilly. I don't doubt your heart on that one. It's the other question I'm worried about. The toughest choice for you, I think, will be deciding whether or not you're going to trust in my love for you."

Gillian laid her head against the solid, comforting warmth

of his chest, feeling the steady rise and fall of his breathing, pondering his words. Max was right. She hadn't believed in him...or in their relationship. Realizing that she had gone back to her old ways frightened her. But Max had forgiven her, and he believed in her and was willing to stick it out, to make their love grow...that was a truth that brought her hope.

"Gillian," he said gently, "a while back, I asked you to make the most important choice of your life, one that would affect you eternally. Now, I'm asking you to do it one more time, to make one more choice—one that will impact the rest of your natural life. I'm asking you to *believe* in me. To believe in love."

Firmly, he grasped her by the shoulders and stepped back, holding her out in front of him where he could see her entire face. "I'm not saying that I'll never fail you," he warned. "But I *am* promising to love you the very best that I can."

Gillian gave him a tremulous smile. "You know, a month ago, I wouldn't have been sure how to answer you," she answered a bit unsteadily. "Two months ago, I'm pretty certain I would have run away. In the past few weeks, though, and even in the past few days, I've learned what it means to let myself be led by God." As she spoke she gathered confidence. Finally, she could meet Max's eyes without feeling a sense of shame. She was healing. She was on her way.

"When I see how much he's changed me already, how he's surprised me in every area of my life, I can believe that there is reason to hope, no matter what lies ahead." Impatiently, she wiped the tears from her eyes, wanting nothing to blur her vision of the man she adored.

"I love you, too, Max!" she said passionately. "I want to learn what it means to know you, and to let you know me. I know there's a risk. But I think...no, I *know* I'm ready. And I'm willing to trust that no matter what happens, God will be with us, helping us through."

With those final words, the last of the questions were answered, the last of the walls torn down. His eyes brimming with tears, Max placed one hand on either side of Gillian's face and stepped in close, so their bodies were almost—but not quite—touching. With breathless anticipation, Gillian watched, wide-eyed, as his face drew ever nearer, anticipating the gentle sweetness of his lips on hers....

"THIS IS THE *LAST* CALL FOR FLIGHT NUMBER FOUR SIX TWO," the once-perky flight attendant announced meaningfully, staring pointedly at the tickets in Gillian's and Max's hands.

Gillian jumped. Max laughed and planted an off-center kiss on the side of her nose, diffusing her look of disappointment by whispering, "Later, my love."

"And now, I believe that's our boarding call." He grinned and waved cheerfully at the airline attendant, indicating that they were on their way. "I don't know about you," he told Gillian confidently, "but I'm looking forward to spending some quality time at the telescope together." Carry-on bags shouldered, they headed for the gate.

Gillian smiled up at the man who had so completely captured her heart, her earlier suffering forgotten. "I'm so glad you're coming, Max!"

He returned the grin. "Me, too. I have a funny feeling you and I may very well be spending the rest of our lives together, gazing at stars," he said. "And I can't wait to begin."

Gillian shook her head seriously and reached up to bestow one more kiss on his cheek before boarding. "Oh no, Max," she told him, her heart brimming with the promise of love. "We've already begun."

Epilogue

Surely he has done great things.
JOEL 2:20
Praise the LORD, O my soul, and forget not all his benefits—
who...crowns you with love and compassion, who
satisfies your desires with good things....
PSALM 103:2-5

One spring morning

"Honey, you up? Gilly? Hon?"

Moaning softly, Gillian withdrew one hand from under the thick down comforter and swatted halfheartedly at the warm breath tickling her ear. "Unnh. Go 'way." She fumbled with the tangerine plaid bedspread, hoping—but failing—to pull it up over her ears before the next attack.

"Hooooooooo-ney," Max softly blew on a tendril of honey-colored hair at her temple, then ended the teasing once and for all with a solid kiss to her ear. "Come on, lazybones. Get up. You've slept half the morning. It's time to wake up and smell the coffee."

Gillian rolled over to face the man sitting beside her on the feather bed, holding a steaming mug of fragrant French roast. She issued a blank stare through sleepy eyes, somehow managing to keep her laughter in check. "You've just been *dying* for me to wake up so you could say that, haven't you?" she asked groggily.

Max grinned and waggled his eyebrows. "*Maaaay*-be. Then

227

again, maybe I've just been dying for you to wake up so I could give you this...." Carefully holding the coffee out to one side of the bed, he leaned in once more—this time seeking out her lips and planting them with a kiss that was gentle, yet held a tantalizing hint of promise.

"Mmm," Gillian said a moment later, smacking her lips. "Tastes like you've already had your coffee."

"That's right," Max agreed, watching her playfully. He began to inch forward once more. "And now I'm going to get some sugar...."

Gillian laughed and squealed and rolled slowly out of reach, watching Max struggle to balance the coffee as the mattress moved under her weight.

"Watcha doin', Mama?" a sweet voice called from the doorway. Gillian sat up and smiled. In her pale-yellow footie pajamas and halo of golden curls, the child resembled a small sun.

"Come here, angel," Gillian said lovingly, and sat up in bed, making room for her daughter's flannel-covered body. She fluffed up two plump pillows and positioned them behind her back. "Oh, not there, sweetie," she said gently, as Emily wriggled up into her lap, poking one tiny elbow against her slightly burgeoning belly.

"Did I hurt the baby?" Emmie asked, moving over slightly but staying within the warm circle of her mother's arms. Her tiny features pinched together in a serious expression.

"No, no. It's okay, Em," Gillian assured her, running her fingers through the child's unruly curls. "I've got quite a bit of padding down there." She laughed and rolled her eyes at Max, who had placed the coffee on the nightstand and was settling down beside them to cuddle with "his girls." "Maybe a little *too* much padding," she complained wryly.

"Now, now. That's just silly." Max leaned down to plant a kiss on the stomach in question. "The doctor said you're right on schedule weight-wise. Besides...you're beautiful."

"Hmm." Gillian pretended not to believe him, but her face was flushed with pleasure.

"Mama?"

"Mmm, yes, sweetheart?"

Emily turned her head and looked up at Gillian with wide eyes the same shade of blue as the sky. "I want to ride my bike," she announced, referring to the cherry-red tricycle she had received for her third birthday. To Emmie, every two-or three-wheeled vehicle was a "bike."

"I think we can do that today," Gillian told her. Across the top of Emmie's head, her eyes met Max's and caught the look of love in them. A soft smile teased her lips and spread across her face as she looked at her beautiful child and then her adoring husband.

Gillian reveled in the feeling of contentment. If only she could have known as a teenager, and as a young woman, what God had in store for her. If only she could have trusted, could have believed. How different her life might have been! How much more joyous....

Such thoughts still came to her as she struggled to come to terms with the life she had once lived. And yet, the realization had recently dawned on her that it was this same life—the life filled with loneliness, anger, and fear—that led her to make the life choices that had placed her in the path of Max: the man who would lead her to the Lord and one day become her husband.

The feeling of sadness was fleeting, her heart surged with delight once again. Perhaps this was yet another manifestation of God's mercy: the realization that all things in life—all choices, all emotions, all failures, all weaknesses—are redeemable by God. The aspects of her life she hated most were the very ones that had ultimately drawn her to God's arms. It was true: all things *did* work to the glory of God for those who loved him. Even for people like her.

"No, Mama," Emily insisted, interrupting her thoughts. "I wanna ride my bike *now.*"

Max grinned. Gillian smiled ruefully. Their little girl certainly was a handful. But she was a lovable handful, a precious handful, and Emmie's parents treasured every minute with her.

"Breakfast first," she informed the child.

"But, Mama—"

"No 'buts,'" Gillian insisted. "And you've got to get dressed and brush your teeth before you can go outside."

"Slave driver," Max whispered in her ear.

Gillian's lips twitched in amusement. "Your father will help you," she said.

Max laughed and kissed Gillian once more—this time on the forehead, for good measure—then scooped up his giggling little girl and swung her around the sun-drenched room before heading off to satisfy Gillian's list of demands.

As Gillian watched them go, a feeling of contentment welled up inside her. The Lord who was able to accomplish great and mighty things had outdone himself when it came to her life. Great were his blessings. Mighty was his grace.

And the words Max had written in her Bible six years ago were true.

It was just the beginning.

Dear Reader,

I am not an astrophysicist. I don't even play one on TV. What I *don't* know about wave function and particle mechanics could (and does) fill entire libraries. And though I have, in *Stardust*, dabbled at exploring this field, my words simply represent one scientifically-challenged woman's understanding of an extremely complex subject.

Wrestling with this topic wasn't easy. But it *was* fascinating...and enlightening. This was a surprise to me, because the creation of the universe was a subject I had always avoided. In high school, I had teachers who swore by evolution and the big bang, two theories I believed to be inconsistent with the Bible's teachings. I was afraid of learning something that might undermine my faith, so I tried to ignore the controversy. Years later, I found that I still had my head buried in the sand.

Unfortunately, this little ostrich act didn't strengthen my faith. On the contrary, it weakened it...considerably. I didn't trust in my ability to discern truth from falsehood. Worst of all, I failed to trust that God's Word would stand up under scientific examination.

When I finally allowed myself to explore the subject, however, I discovered an abundance of scientific evidence that supports a biblical creation of the universe. I won't presume to claim that my characters' beliefs are correct (although the theory discussed in *Stardust* comes from the scientific community and is one possible explanation). Nor will I tell you which of the many theories to believe. But I can tell you that if, like me, you have ever longed for scientific reasoning to support your biblical views (or vice versa), there's plenty of it out there.

I had a lot of fun learning about astronomy. But the best part of the process was being reminded that God is faithful—even when I don't trust him to be. I'm finding that whatever answers I seek, God can help me find them. All I have to do is ask...then open my eyes, and see what he has to show me.

"Ask, and it shall be given to you; seek, and you shall find; knock, and it shall be opened to you. For everyone who asks receives, and he who seeks finds, and to him who knocks it shall be opened" Matthew 7:7-8.

PALISADES...PURE ROMANCE

⤳ PALISADES ⤳

Reunion, Karen Ball
Refuge, Lisa Tawn Bergren
Torchlight, Lisa Tawn Bergren
Treasure, Lisa Tawn Bergren
Chosen, Lisa Tawn Bergren
Firestorm, Lisa Tawn Bergren
Wise Man's House, Melody Carlson
Arabian Winds, Linda Chaikin (Premier)
Cherish, Constance Colson
Chase the Dream, Constance Colson (Premier)
Angel Valley, Peggy Darty
Sundance, Peggy Darty
Moonglow, Peggy Darty (June, 1997)
Love Song, Sharon Gillenwater
Antiques, Sharon Gillenwater
Song of the Highlands, Sharon Gillenwater (Premier)
Texas Tender, Sharon Gillenwater (June, 1997)
Secrets, Robin Jones Gunn
Whispers, Robin Jones Gunn
Echoes, Robin Jones Gunn
Sunsets, Robin Jones Gunn
Clouds, Robin Jones Gunn (July, 1997)
Coming Home, Barbara Jean Hicks
Snow Swan, Barbara Jean Hicks
Irish Eyes, Annie Jones
Glory, Marilyn Kok
Sierra, Shari MacDonald
Forget-Me-Not, Shari MacDonald
Diamonds, Shari MacDonald

Stardust, Shari MacDonald
Westward, Amanda MacLean
Stonehaven, Amanda MacLean
Everlasting, Amanda MacLean
Promise Me the Dawn, Amanda MacLean (Premier)
Kingdom Come, Amanda MacLean
Betrayed, Lorena McCourtney
Escape, Lorena McCourtney
Dear Silver, Lorena McCourtney
Voyage, Elaine Schulte

ANTHOLOGIES

A Christmas Joy, Darty, Gillenwater, MacLean
Mistletoe, Ball, Hicks, McCourtney
A Mother's Love, Bergren, Colson, MacLean

THE PALISADES LINE

*Ask for them at your local bookstore. If the title you seek is not in stock,
the store may order you a copy using the ISBN listed.*

Wise Man's House, Melody Carlson
ISBN 1-57673-070-0
Kestra McKenzie, a young widow trying to make a new life for herself, thinks she
has found the solidity she longs for when she purchases her childhood dream
house—a stone mansion on the Oregon Coast. Just as renovations begin, a mysterious stranger moves into her caretaker's cottage—and into her heart.

Moonglow, Peggy Darty (June, 1997)
ISBN 1-57673-112-X
During the Summer Olympics set in Atlanta, Tracy Kosell comes back to her
hometown of Moonglow, Georgia, to investigate the disappearance of a wealthy
socialite. She meets up with former schoolmate Jay Calloway, who's one of the
detectives assigned to the case. As their attraction grows and the mercury rises,
they unwrap a case that isn't as simple as it seemed.

Texas Tender, Sharon Gillenwater (June, 1997)
ISBN 1-57673-111-1
When Shelby Nolan inherits a watermelon farm, she moves from Houston to a
small west Texas town. Spotting two elderly men digging holes in her field each
night, she turns to neighbor Deputy Sheriff Logan Slade to figure out what's
going on. Together they uncover a long-buried robbery and discover the fulfill-
ment of their own dreams.

Clouds, Robin Jones Gunn (July, 1997)
ISBN 1-57673-113-8
On a trip to Germany, flight attendant Shelly Graham unexpectedly runs into her
old boyfriend, Jonathan Renfield. Since she still cares for him, it's hard for Shelly
to hide her hurt when she learns he's engaged. It isn't until she goes to meet
friends in Glenbrooke, Oregon, that they meet again—and this time, they're both
ready to be honest.

Sunsets, Robin Jones Gunn
ISBN 1-57673-103-0
Alissa Benson loves her job as a travel agent. But when the agency has computer
problems, they call in expert Brad Phillips. Alissa can't wait for Brad to fix the
computers and leave—he's too blunt for her comfort. So she's more than a little
upset when she moves into a duplex and finds out he's her neighbor!

Snow Swan, Barbara Jean Hicks
ISBN 1-57673-107-3
Life hasn't been easy for Toni Ferrier. As an unwed mother and a recovering alcoholic, she doesn't feel worthy of anyone's love. Then she meets Clark McConaughey, who helps her launch her business aboard the sternwheeler Snow Swan. Sparks fly between them, but if Clark finds out the truth about Toni's past, will he still love her?

Irish Eyes, Annie Jones
ISBN 1-57673-108-1
When Julia Reed finds a young boy, who claims to be a leprechaun, camped out under a billboard, she gets drawn into a century-old crime involving a real pot of gold. Interpol agent Cameron O'Dea is trying to solve the crime. In the process, he takes over the homeless shelter that Julia runs, camps out in her neighbor's RV, and generally turns her life upside down!

Stardust, Shari MacDonald
ISBN 1-57673-109-X
As a teenager, Gillian Spencer fell in love with astronomy...and with Max Bishop. But after he leaves her heartbroken, she learns to keep her feelings guarded. Now that she's a graduate student studying astronomy, she thinks she has left the past far behind. So when she gets an exciting assignment, she's shocked to learn she's been paired with the now-famous Dr. Maxwell Bishop.

Kingdom Come, Amanda MacLean
ISBN 1-57673-120-0
In 1902, feisty Ivy Rose Clayborne, M.D., returns to her hometown of Kingdom Come to fight the coal mining company that is ravaging the land. She meets an unexpected ally, a man who claims to be a drifter but in reality is Harrison MacKenzie, grandson of the coal mining baron. Together they face the aftermath of betrayal, the fight for justice...and the price of love.

Dear Silver, Lorena McCourtney
ISBN 1-57673-110-3
When Silver Sinclair receives a polite but cold letter from Chris Bentley ending their relationship, she's shocked, since she's never met the man! She confronts Chris about his insensitive attitude toward this other Silver Sinclair, and finds herself becoming friends with a man who's unlike anyone she's ever met.

A Mother's Love, Bergren, Colson, MacLean
Three popular Palisades authors bring you heartwarming stories about the joys and challenges of romance in the midst of motherhood.
By Lisa Bergren: A widower and his young daughter go to Southern California for vacation, and return with much more than they expected.

By Constance Colson: Cassie Jenson wants her old sweetheart to stay in her memories. But when he moves back to town, they find out that they could never forget each other.

By Amanda MacLean: A couple is expecting their first baby, and they hardly have enough time for each other. With the help of an old journal and a last-minute getaway, they work to rekindle their love.

෴

PALISADES PREMIER
More Story. More Romance.

Arabian Winds, Linda Chaikin
ISBN 1-57673-3-105-7
In the first book of the trilogy, World War I is breaking upon the deserts of Arabia in 1914. Young nurse Allison Wescott is on holiday with an archaeological club, but a murder interrupts her plans, and a mysterious officer keeps turning up wherever she goes!
Watch for more books in Linda Chaikin's Egypt series!

Song of the Highlands, Sharon Gillenwater
ISBN 1-57673-946-4
During the Napoleonic Wars, Kiernan is a piper, but he comes back to find out he's inherited a title. At his run-down estate, he meets the beautiful Mariah. During a trip to London, they face a kidnapping...and discover their love for each other.
Watch for more books in Sharon Gillenwater's Scottish series!

෴

We're excited to announce a new line:
PASSAGES
Romance, mystery, comedy...Real life.

Homeward, Melody Carlson (July, 1997)
ISBN 1-57673-029-8
When Meg Lancaster learns that her grandmother is dying, she returns to the small town on the Oregon coast where she spent vacations as a child. After being away for twenty years, the town hasn't changed...but her family has. Meg struggles with her memories of the past and what is now reality, until tragedy strikes the family and she must learn to face the future.

Redeeming Love, Francine Rivers (July, 1997)
ISBN 1-57673-186-3

The only men Angel has ever known have betrayed her. When she meets Michael Hosea in the gold country of California, she has no reason to believe he's any different. But Michael is different. And through him Angel learns what love really means—the kind of love that can wipe away the shame of her past.

Enough! Gayle Roper (August, 1997)
ISBN 1-57673-185-5

When Molly Gregory gets fed up with her three teenaged children, she announces that she's going on strike. She and her husband Pete stand back and watch as chaos results in their household, in a hilarious experiment that teaches their children how to honor their parents.